Palgrave Hate Studies

Series Editors
Neil Chakraborti
Department of Criminology
University of Leicester
Leicester, UK

Barbara Perry
Faculty of Social Science and Humanities
University of Ontario
Oshawa, ON, Canada

This series builds on recent developments in the broad and interdisciplinary field of hate studies. Palgrave Hate Studies aims to bring together in one series the very best scholars who are conducting hate studies research around the world. Reflecting the range and depth of research and scholarship in this burgeoning area, the series welcomes contributions from established hate studies researchers who have helped to shape the field, as well as new scholars who are building on this tradition and breaking new ground within and outside the existing canon of hate studies research.

More information about this series at
http://www.palgrave.com/gp/series/14695

David Wilkin

Disability Hate Crime

Experiences of Everyday Hostility on Public Transport

palgrave
macmillan

David Wilkin
Department of Criminology
University of Leicester
Leicester, UK

Palgrave Hate Studies
ISBN 978-3-030-28725-2 ISBN 978-3-030-28726-9 (eBook)
https://doi.org/10.1007/978-3-030-28726-9

This Palgrave Pivot imprint is published by the registered company Springer Nature Switzerland AG.
The registered company address is: Gewerbestrasse 11, 6330 Cham, Switzerland

This work is dedicated to those who have given their dignity on a daily basis to get to where they need to be. Everyone will hopefully enjoy a better public transport experience, someday.

Foreword

I am honoured to have been asked to write the Foreword for this much-needed book on disability hate crime on public transport. Its publication cannot come soon enough. Within the United Kingdom (UK), 7226 disability hate crimes were recorded by the police in England and Wales in 2017–18, which was not only an increase of 30% compared to the previous year but also a continuation of an upward trend since 2012–13, with recorded rates having more than quadrupled in that time frame.

It is widely acknowledged, however, that police-recorded figures are a considerable underestimate of the actual number of hate crimes taking place within the UK. The Crime Survey for England and Wales—which provides an alternative measure of hate crime victimisation accounting for those incidents that were not reported to the police—estimated that 52,000 disability hate crimes took place within 2017–18. This presents an alarming picture of how often victims of disability hate crime suffer in silence and how few incidents come to the attention of the police.

In response to the growing awareness of the problems posed by disability hate crime, we have seen the implementation of policy and practice which is designed to afford protection to those affected by it. The most recent Criminal Justice Joint Inspection on the handling of cases involving disability hate crime highlights that there have been significant improvements in relation to the investigation and prosecution of this monitored strand. While interest in disability hate crime has steadily increased within the context of scholarship, there is still much that we do not know in terms of the lived realities of hate crime victimisation for those who are targeted on the basis of their learning difficulties, their physical disabilities and/or their mental ill-health.

David's book provides an unflinching, harrowing and nuanced account of the hostility, harassment and violence faced by disabled people on public transport—an environment which has received very little scholarly attention in relation to hate crime. It is difficult to comprehend the sadness, the fear, the humiliation and the sense of isolation which many disabled people experience while undertaking what for most people is a mundane activity. This research, which illustrates the value of adopting an innovative and flexible methodological approach, not only makes a significant contribution to the field of hate studies but, importantly, has 'real-world' implications. David puts forward a set of achievable and evidence-based recommendations which if implemented have the capacity to enable public transport providers and professionals to deliver a service in which disabled people feel welcome, safe and supported.

Leicester, UK Stevie-Jade Hardy

Preface

Being disabled has for years been about overcoming barriers to lead a normal life. Barriers can be governmental, physical cultural or simply barriers of non-understanding. Who is, or is not, disabled is often defined by the wheelchair. This wheelchair, especially in its pictogram form, has become the symbol of disability. However, this symbol does not represent those with hidden disabilities, for example, facial peculiarities, communications problems, mental challenges, or those with lifelong conditions which require extensive monitoring and medication. The symbol is not representative of people who have chronic pain to the extent that every step is part of a planned process of ambulation. What pictogram could ever represent those who suffer in silence with hidden conditions?

Aside from these societal barriers, what else could go wrong? Why should an already-difficult life get worse? Why would people choose to denigrate, abuse and potentially destroy the lives of others who are already struggling? Public transport is a necessity for many people. To use it is to associate closely with strangers in a small space for a sometimes indeterminate length of time, often without any information and in circumstances which can become frustrating. Add to this mix a disability, hidden or otherwise, which makes travel a daily mountain to climb; the preparation, the planning and the sheer effort of doing it. Now factor-in an abuser, someone who seems to gain pleasure from attacking your identity and making you feel worthless. Then others join in, a barrage of abusive, caustic and violent statements and actions which make you wonder if life is worth living. Is this a nightmare? No! For me and for many of the contributors to my book, this is real and it is every day. Long after the actuality of the experience, the ignominy continues to live on.

This book is written to represent a very personal research journey to unmask episodes of hostility. In doing so, it reveals other personal journeys taken by people, my participants, and their journeys on UK public transport. These are sometimes enjoyable, often tortuous and occasionally thoroughly unpleasant. Please note that whilst the author would have preferred to use the social model of disability and the person-first reference of 'people with disabilities' it was felt appropriate to use terms recognised by the police and other agencies within the UK. Therefore, the medical model of disability and the terms disabled people/victims are used.

Leicester, UK David Wilkin

Acknowledgements

My heartfelt thanks to the following people for the gracious help extended to me despite themselves having busy schedules:

Thank you to Bev Wilkin for your patience, support and caring. Thank you for the flapjacks which opened doors and were consumed all over the UK including within the police, academia and government circles. Thank you also for distributing flyers and being a professional participant recruiter. With further thanks for your clear thinking!

Thank you to my PhD supervisors: Prof Stevie-Jade Hardy and Prof Neil Chakraborti at the Centre for Hate Studies, Department of Criminology within the University of Leicester for your enduring professionalism and patience. Evidence, if it were required, that hard work always pays off.

Thank you to my mum and dad, now in a different world, you nearly gave up on me and I don't blame you—but you didn't and that took strength.

For all participants and focus group members and enablers, thank you for your time, patience and candour.

For one of my participants, now deceased, who during his honoured military career was twice-knighted, a former submarine commander and Rear Admiral. He was latterly reduced to tears after being repeatedly abused on buses—for being in a wheelchair and taking up space.

Thank you to the officials from public transport authorities and those staff for the time that you generously sacrificed.

For all the tears which I have shed and have been shed on the part of all of my courageous participants who face inhuman awfulness almost every day.

For Abi

Contents

About the Author

I didn't understand my diagnosis of being autistic. I thought that it had something to do with being able to paint—although I was no artist. Having avoided going to school for almost five years because of the bullying and hostility faced getting there—on public transport—and at school, I left school not being able to construct a sentence or knowing what grammar was. I could however complete an application form and a 31 career in public transport provision at all levels began. From the *front line* to senior management, the unacceptable face of some members of the travelling public was a constant reminder of how inexplicable some people can be in their behaviour. The man who refused to leave a burning train because he had yet to finish his newspaper, the woman who thought that that people should commit suicide at weekends so as not to delay her weekday commute and the woman who demanded that the train with a brake failure should run because she had an appointment. There were also incidents which impacted on disabled passengers: the man in the wheelchair being tipped onto the electrified track, and the visually impaired man who had a plastic bag placed over his head and was spun around. These were sickening incidents that I had witnessed and managed.

Following retirement, I took a career-turn. This involved being a voluntary worker with Essex County Council finding work for disadvantaged people and working with the UK National Health Service as a volunteer. Some years prior to this, the author had gained two undergraduate degrees from the UK-based Open University where no formal qualifications were needed to enter. An MSc in criminology followed at the University of Leicester and then a PhD focusing on hate crimes against disabled people on public transport. Having been a victim and then a witness to incidents against disabled people before studying the criminality attached to hate perpetration, it seemed that the next logical step was to write about it. I sincerely hope that you are enlightened by this book.

CHAPTER 1

Introduction: Exploring Disability Hate Crime

Abstract This chapter introduces the monograph. In doing this, it outlines the author's recent research into disability hate crime and the motivation behind it. Whilst the particular focus of the author's work was to understand the hostility enacted against disabled people through a focus on UK public transport, the chapter also explains how hate crime is defined in the UK. The nuances of disability hate crime are presented along with the two most recognised models of disability used. An overview of crime on public transport in general terms is given before the structure of the monograph is presented. The chapter is about breaking new ground. Research of this nature has mainly been avoided to date as has the routine inclusion of disabled people in research. It was the personal and academic aspirations of the author which drove this project as well as the unearthing of the plight of some disabled passengers.

Keywords Disability • Hate crime • Research • Academia

1.1 The Motivation

I recall with warmth the July of 1969. My parents allowed me to stay up late to watch the Moon landings on TV. I had already posted my schoolboy-handwritten application to become an astronaut to NASA (the National Aeronautics and Space Administration in the US). Although I did not get a response, I was a happy eight-year-old with aspirations to explore the stars

D. Wilkin, *Disability Hate Crime*, Palgrave Hate Studies,
https://doi.org/10.1007/978-3-030-28726-9_1

and shake hands with alien life forms. My life had changed by 1973; however, I was sitting in a corner of an upstairs room at home looking down out of a window upon society below and hoping that nobody could see me. My hands shook uncontrollably and I had already attempted suicide for the first time. Any friends seemed as far away as the Moon, and I very much wanted to die.

In the late 1960s, I had been diagnosed as autistic. Although this meant little to me, I began to notice that I looked different from others. It hardly made any difference to my life until I started at a school which I travelled to by bus and train. During those tortuous journeys, I was ridiculed, spat at and beaten up. My head had been used as a football in the playground, and a cricket bat swung at it in an experiment to see how much damage could be done to it. I was paying the price of being different. My parents were loving but poor. Although frequently washed, my school blazer always showed faint traces of the chalked branding applied to it by bullies and evidence of the rivers of spit which had run down it. I never had the courage to explain why I frequently came home in this condition or how I felt. I never could explain why I found excluding myself from society, missing years of schooling through truanting and even trying to kill myself, was preferable to facing any more of this torment. Although I didn't know it at the time, I was the victim of acts which latterly became broadly recognised as hate crimes.

Aside from being an astronaut, my other dream was to be a train driver. Then, the standard required to complete the application form was low, low enough for me to be accepted. I later became a train driver/instructor—the dream job. I had a long career in public transport at all levels, and I had seen the public at its best and its drunken worst. I had been instrumental in the deaths of two people who used my train as a tool for suicide. I had also been an incident manager where I witnessed many incidents including those of hate crimes against disabled people—some with horrific outcomes. Other roles included designing and delivering equality and inclusion training. Following retirement, I became a criminologist and was later appointed as a Lead Coordinator of the Disability Hate Crime Network in the UK. These life-events had ignited a passion to research the topic of disability hate crime (DHC). Through this book, I hope to take you on a journey from a rudimentary understanding of hate crime and the concept of disability to finding out how this research was undertaken. In doing so, I will share my findings to reveal the horror of everyday abuse on UK public transport. I will also disclose that those who are charged with safeguarding disabled people using public transport in the UK have mainly been failing to do so, a factor which has led to some people choosing to exclude themselves from society rather than face the wrath of this everyday abuse. Having been a victim, it would be a reasonable aspiration to want to research the entire geography of where hostility towards disabled people occurs. However, this would have been inconceivable for a solo, self-funded researcher. Instead, the social microcosm of public transport not only provided a familiar environment for me to study but also one which could be representative of other public theatres where abuse takes place.

1.2 The Research

Aside from the personal motivation for this research, there is a wider need. Academics have focused relatively little on disability hate crime and have not concerned themselves with hate crime on public transport (Chakraborti 2015). This is despite these spaces being recognised as risk-laden environments for those who are perceived to be different (Equality and Human Rights Commission [EHRC] 2011; Home Office 2016). The research that I undertook was through a PhD project in 2017–19 which aimed to develop a nuanced understanding of how disability hate crime (DHC) is experienced on public transport. I thought I knew what it was to be a victim, but this research journey was to unveil so much else.

The research objectives were:

- To consider the dynamics between victims, perpetrators and bystanders on public transport.
- To assess which public transport modes pose a greater risk for victims of DHC.
- To explore the impacts of DHC on public transport.
- To examine the ways in which public transport providers and front-line staff respond to DHC on public transport.
- To use research evidence to develop a series of recommendations for policy and practice to improve responses to DHC on public transport.

1.3 What Is Hate Crime?

Often discussed and derided but little understood there is a need to understand what hate crime is. One academic definition of hate crime is:

> Acts of violence, hostility and intimidation directed towards people because of their identity or perceived 'difference'. (Chakraborti et al. 2014)

Or we could use the UK police definition hate incident, a hate crime being one which additionally incurs a criminal offence having been conducted:

> Any incident, which may or may not constitute a criminal offence, which is perceived by the victim or any other person, as being motivated by hostility or prejudice. (College of Policing [CoP] 2014:3–4)

At the time that this book is being written in 2019, in the UK, a nation where hate crime is beginning to be understood and accepted, there are five recognised and monitored strands of hate crime (CoP 2014). These are sexual orientation hate crime, transgender hate crime, racial hate crime, religious hate crime and disability or disablist hate crime.[1] Each of these strands continues to be susceptible to hostility, and therefore, they deserve additional protection from society. These strands are categorisations which apply and provide consistency across the UK police and criminal justice agencies (Home Office 2016). Such typification should ensure that hate offences are *flagged*, that is distinguished, from the moment of reporting to the police, through the charging process, to the courtroom. Police guidance in the UK advises police officers to record the incident as a hate crime if so demanded by the complainant (CoP 2014). This flagging is designed to raise awareness of the higher personal impact which potentially befalls the victim and to signal, later in the process, the higher sentencing provisions which are available to the judiciary. There has been much progress concerning legislation in the UK including the availability of sentencing uplifts in court if disability hate motivation is proven. There is also realisation that this legislation does not go far enough and this has led to a review of that law by the UK-based professional body of legal professionals *The Law Commission*, which commenced in 2019.

Despite such progress, not all offences are recorded as hate offences. The term hate crime is not always a readily accepted one. In the 1990s, when hate crime was developing as a concept in the US, Jacobs and Potter (1997) were presenting an antithesis to any particular recognition of hate crime. They argued that hate crimes would be difficult to distinguish, to prosecute, and that hate motivations would be problematic to ascertain.

[1] This book utilises the term disability hate crime. The term disablist hate crime implies that perpetrators have an inherent disablist prejudice which may motivate their hostilities against disabled people. As during the underlying research this premise was not evidenced then this book will avoid that assumption.

Indeed, to prove that a hate offence has been enacted in the UK needs more than merely a suspicion. Instead, a definite indication in the actions or language of the offender is needed to illustrate hate motivation. Indeed, the word *hate* itself may be problematic. The words *bias* or *prejudice* may inform this area of offending more. Nonetheless, in the UK, the notification of a hate incident or crime is one initiated by the victim or witness, and the police are obliged to record it as such.

But to focus entirely on purely formal definitions would be to limit our understanding of hate crime to prescribed proclamations. To do so would be to obscure the emotion, the anger and the fear that hate crimes produce. As I know to my cost, to be a victim of a hate attack is to have your very identity challenged and ridiculed. Everything that you are, or have striven to achieve, becomes the target of someone else's mission to humiliate, frighten and destabilise you. It feels like your abusers are destroying any value which you have to society—to satisfy their gratification. The result of this is that it wears you down. You start to believe what they say that you have no value, no use and no purpose. There ultimately becomes no point in you continuing to live. These attacks could happen to anyone who is perceived as being different; that difference is the spur to acts of personal and caustic condemnation.

So why do hate crimes deserve a specific focus? Hate crimes are personal; they are a direct attack on a person's identity. Whilst the theft of a car or stealing money might produce material benefits for the thief, a hate attack is a direct attempt to assault a person's identity and devalue them and their humanity. As well as the attack on an individual's characteristics, evidence shows that hate crimes are often everyday occurrences. Not necessarily spawned from hatred, but instead they can be the products of routine misunderstanding, overflowing emotions, inappropriate humour—sometimes referred to as banter—or representative of bias (Iganski 2008a, b). Whatever the motivation, evidence has also shown that hate crime has a deep and long-term psychological effect on its victims and witnesses (Iganski and Lagou 2015). Psychological disorder and fear exist long after any offence has been committed—as I can testify to. Even in later life, an unwillingness to report such offences remains, either out of embarrassment or perhaps a fear of reprisal. If courage has been found to report incidents, evidence suggests that police officers may be reticent to process reports of hate crime (Her Majesties Inspectorate of Constabulary and Fire & Rescue Services [HMICFRS] 2018). The police service has not always seen the processing and investigation of hate crimes as *true policing*.

Cultures have existed in police forces which enforce a hierarchy of crime where acts of violence are at the top and hate offences lie near the bottom (Bowling 1999; Hall 2010). In summary, hate crime is different in its motivation, its victim impact and its effect-longevity. But one of those five monitored strands, disability hate crime, has its own particular nuances.

1.4 Disability Hate Crime

Disability hate crimes are offences against people who are different because they have one or more disabilities. These might be physical, psychological, personal mannerisms or other difficulties, for example, in communicating effectively. Many disabled people incur comorbidity of conditions thus magnifying difficulty and exposure to the risk of hostility. In the UK, the legal definition of disability encompasses a wide set of impairments:

> ...
>
> You are disabled under the Equality Act 2010 if you have a physical or mental impairment that has a 'substantial' and 'long-term' negative effect on your ability to do normal daily activities.
>
> ...
>
> (Equality Act 2010: Schedule One, Part One, 2(2))

This definition delineates a long-term effect as impairment lasting, or likely to last, more than 12 months or if the impairment is likely to re-occur (ibid., 2(1)). Furthermore, cancer, multiple sclerosis, HIV and temporarily debilitating conditions are included in the description (ibid., 6(1)). Disabilities which are no longer causing impairment also continue to be recognised under the Equality Act.

1.5 Why Specifically Recognise Disability Hate Crime?

Disability hate crimes have an immediate and a lasting impact which compounds any difficulties already affecting disabled people. Personal accounts of this are revealed in Chaps. 3 and 4. In revealing these, public transport is an exemplary environment. If a disabled person requires the use of public transport, then it is surely demanding enough for a person to need to meticulously plan journeys, pack equipment, food and medicines. Complicating this daunting prospect further is the need to navigate the complexities of sometimes crowded, often poor-performing; public transport services and journeys can be unbearable. Finally, add to this combination the expectation that some disabled people will have to circumnavigate a gamut of routine hostility and the entire venture becomes a formidable one. As will be revealed through the experiences exposed in this book, any journey is potentially a nightmare experience and a nightmare that is likely to be repeated.

The recognition of disability hate crime as an explicit crime was highlighted in the UK in 2007. Fiona Pilkington took her own life and that of her daughter Frankie after them being victims to years of supposedly unremarkable abuse. Fiona, clearly caught in a desperate situation, placed her daughter and herself in a car which Fiona then set on fire. Her situation must have been terrifyingly unendurable. Their social isolation and susceptibility to disability-related hate offences, alongside other anti-social behaviours, underwrote this tragic case. The local police were found to be lacking professionalism in their responses to calls for help (Independent Police Complaints Commission [IPCC][2] 2011). The IPCC report into this police conduct found a succession of incidents of apparently low-level, unlinked, anti-social offences which the police failed to deal with. The police viewed these being as a result of Pilkington's supposed *vulnerability* rather than recognising Pilkington's required protection and justice. This perception of vulnerability is a key characteristic of precluding disability hate crime victims from being accorded justice (Chakraborti et al. 2014).

Aside from reporting difficulties and not being recognised as deserving of criminal justice, other distinctions apply to victims of disability hate crime. Victims can be particularly susceptible to *mate crime*, where an abuser ostensibly befriends the victim in order to exploit them. This can result in the victim's residence being usurped or possibly their welfare benefits being stolen (Sin 2015). The victim may be reticent to end this acquaintance as friendships are more likely among disabled people to be uncommon. Disabled people are additionally susceptible to being a victim of *cuckooing* (ibid., 2015). This is where an abuser takes up residence with the victim to exploit their home for drug dealing or other wrongdoings. In either case the disabled person may find difficulty in being able to report such an incident due to the perpetrator exerting control over the victim. Alternatively, the victim may cherish the companionship of the offender—no matter how exploitative it may be. Victims of disability hate

[2] Renamed Independent Office for Police Conduct (IOPC), 8 January 2018.

crime are also more likely to be repeat victims, victimised closer to where they live and mistreated by those close to them, for example, by friends, carers and family members (EHRC 2011). The latter point further illustrates why disabled victims may be reticent to report incidents of hate crime. The only people that they regularly see might be that carer or family member. To report any abuse could potentially sever this contact altogether, and that might be an unwanted risk.

As will be detailed in Chap. 3 and 4, everyday abuse befalling disabled people can be an expectation, a norm. This everyday abuse might be delivered as supposedly harmless belittling, mockery or humour on the part of the abuser. A comment about the smell in the room or asking how wheelchair-using females can successfully have a baby may seem like humorous jibes. But these are often received as hurtful, caustic attacks on the victim's disabilities. The disabled people I engaged with as part of my research were often reminded by others that they were a nuisance, were taking up too much space or were wasting the nation's resources. Whilst these comments were occasionally couched in humour, they were threatening and conveyed malice. Other comments were made to disabled people offering judgements as to the social value of the victim. Shouting, threatening and abusive behaviour were used to highlight the apparent worthlessness of the victim and how time consuming it is for the people who have to care for them. Furthermore, these comments were often made publicly along with criticisms about how much social welfare benefit that the victim was receiving or how much trouble they were causing the carer. This book additionally brings to light the carers and friends of disabled people who used the disabled person as a target of social judgementalism. Some carers would speak to other passengers on public transport about—and not to—the disabled person. Indicating how difficult they were to keep clean, how moody they can get and how they had *little accidents*. Behaviour which reduces dignity and devalues the disabled victim.

Disability hate crime victims have further difficulties when reporting hate crime. If they can physically access a police station, and if they have their claim of being a victim of a hate offence effortlessly accepted, they then further face having their testimony not being believed anywhere on the road towards justice (HMICFRS 2018). Disabled people are sometimes also seen as being incapable of making an accurate report (Mind 2007). Furthermore, a perception of *vulnerability* applying to the victim may be common to both the abuser and to those in the criminal justice system.

The abuser may use this perception-to-action offensive behaviour, seeing the victim as an easy target, whilst the latter might use it to avoid steering the victim towards obtaining rightful justice (EHRC 2011).

From the supposedly humorous and misguided abuse of disabled people, there are also incidents of stronger verbalised attacks brought to light within this book. The reason for the very existence of the victim has been challenged by abusers. Victims have been told that they have no purpose in this world and should not therefore continue to live in it. Victims are reminded that they are not wanted on the bus, to catch another bus or that they are better suited to using special services where they do not have to associate with *normal people*. This abuse has been seen to develop into physical hostility. Disabled victims using public transport have been spat at, pushed, punched, kicked and had their equipment confiscated. Some victims have had their sticks pulled; their wheelchairs used as footrests and even had their wheelchair or equipment thrown off of a bus or train. Such is the breadth of the abuse found by my research, and such is the horror faced by some disabled passengers that it remains incredible that the topic of disability hate crime on public transport has not previously been the focus of research.

1.6 Models of Disability

An earlier section of this chapter referred to the UK legal definition of disability. This definition is based on the explanatory *medical model of disability*, and this is commonly used across the criminal justice system and support agencies in the UK (Cameron 2014a). The medical model acknowledges that diagnosis of a disability is made by a professional agent, for example, a medical practitioner, and that this diagnosis can allow access to specialised help and to welfare benefits. To be disabled within this model is to have your disability considered not *normal*, you are someone in need of help and assistance—you are therefore *vulnerable* (ibid., 2014a). The medical model is currently the dominant model within Western society and implies that the disabled person is needy, frail and unable to fully contribute to society. This view of disability is supported by the implication of abnormality prescribed by the World Health Organisation's International Classification of Impairments, Disabilities and Handicaps:

> Disability: any restriction or lack (resulting from impairment) of ability to perform an activity in the manner or within the range considered normal for

a human being. (World Health Organisation [WHO] 1980, cited in Barnes and Mercer 2010:20)

Many disabled people and support organisations however deem this model to be unhelpful (ibid., 2014a) as it places barriers which impede the development of the disabled person.

An alternative model began to emerge in the 1970s. This is the *social model of disability* and is a model which helps empower a person with a disability. It advocates that people are not *disabled* as such but instead they are merely *impaired* and that it is society and its social attitudes which place incapacities upon the impaired person. The social model asserts that society should provide guidance and facilities so that people with disabilities can be empowered to enjoy as full a lifestyle as is possible (Cameron 2014b). Whilst this model ideologically enhances the lives of people with impairments, in times of austerity however it may be too costly or impractical to deliver this modality of care to individuals. Furthermore, it is not the model currently recognised by health or criminal justice agencies in the UK. It is because of this latter point that this book will utilise the medical model of disability which remains in common, if contested, use.

1.7 The Necessity of Public Transport Use

Research by the Papworth Trust (2016) reveals that 57% of disabilities involve restricted mobility. A study by the European Parliament (2015) shows that mobility problems are the root causes of social exclusion for many disabled people. Disabled people are additionally less likely to own, or be able to drive, a car. Therefore, many disabilities have the effect of limiting the potential for a disabled person to gain access to medical, educational and employment opportunities. The European Parliament report also reveals that people with disabilities are at a 30% higher risk of being in poverty and at a higher risk of needing to rely on public transport. Consequently, they are additionally exposed to any variations in the level and efficiency of public service provided. Delbosc and Currie (2011) asserted that reliable public transport, which the disabled passenger has the confidence to use, is fundamental to a disabled person for access to work, education and employment and consequently to their well-being. However, they also claim that reliance on public transport can leave disabled people at a transport disadvantage in that they are limited to the services which are provided for them. People with disabilities can therefore become 'transit captives' (Sung-suk et al. 2014:197).

As well as relying on publicly shared transport, disabled people can have a fractious relationship with fellow passengers. Because of mobility issues and the equipment required for their journey, some disabled people need to use priority spaces or seats, utilise access ramps or operate alarm and assistance buttons. Moreover, movement within these, often cramped, vehicles can lead to the disturbance of other passengers. A requirement to use these spaces or the need to ask others to move has led to contestation, abuse and even physical violence. Incidents of this nature will be illustrated in Chap. 3. Subsequently, because of the reoccurrence of this everyday type of abuse, many disabled people have been dissuaded from using public transport at all. This reluctance, to avoid continuing to be a victim of abuse and intimidation, results in restrictions to their lifestyles. Staying at home has become the preferred option for many at the cost of not being able to attend important medical and other appointments, and routine choices become limited in that social and creative pastimes cannot be enjoyed.

In the UK there has been an ongoing discussion regarding the single-staffing of public transport especially around safety issues, including the safeguarding of passengers. Many trains, buses and Tubes are driver-only operated, and this has been an operational concept in use on UK railways since 1963. It has been the focus of several positive safety reviews (BBC Online 1963; Rail Technology Magazine 2017). Nevertheless no evidence came to light in my research suggesting that a second member of staff would have made a significant positive difference in any of the incidents related to me by participants.

1.8 Crime on Public Transport

Risk of exposure to crime is increased when using public transport (Beecroft and Pangbourne 2014). Furthermore, public transport has been widely reported as being a known trigger environment for hostility and hate offences against people with disabilities (Chakraborti et al. 2014; EHRC 2011; Home Office 2016). Despite this raft of evidence, scholarship concerning hate crime on public transport itself is relatively rare. As long ago as 2000, Clarke and Smith (2000) argued that public transport is an exceptional location for many types of crime because of the vehicular environments, the crowded nature of station spaces and sparse supervision from staff. Routine Activity Theorists within criminology would no doubt agree that opportunities for crime perpetration are readily found in these environments (e.g., see Felson 2002; Iganski 2008b). Routine Activity

Theory requires a victim, an offender and a reduction in *capable guardianship* for that victim. The assessment to attack on the part of the offender would involve an evaluation of that capable guardianship. In other words, the offender would determine that the potential victim and others nearby were ill-prepared to mount a defence of the victim. That the victim is possibly uncomfortable or confused in a busy place like a subway or bus station is a further factor which might reduce a victim's confidence to defend themselves (Reynald 2010). There may also be insufficient staff members or surveillance systems to deter such acts. Many of us may be able to recall our frustration and feelings of vulnerability at being lost and without assistance when using public transport interchanges.

Clarke and Smith (2000) asserted that public transport providers however cannot afford, with their constricted profit margins, to let crime thrive on their systems. Designing-out crime, or reinforcing crime prevention, therefore becomes an imperative. Some of the crimes Clarke and Smith discussed as being predicated on public transport were: sexual assault/harassment; pickpocketing; public nuisances and anti-social behaviour. To safeguard people against crime, Clarke and Smith recommend several solutions. These suggestions included: raised staffing levels to provide vigilance and assistance where necessary; installing alarm systems within buses and trams and the use of closed-circuit television (CCTV) with digital recording facilities and providing real-time travel information. The latter, for example, would result in passengers having to spend less time lingering at bus stops not knowing when the next bus was due. On UK public transport, many buses and trains are now fitted with CCTV which is digitally recorded, and these fitments are now seen as standard and essential for the protection of both passengers and staff. As an example of current policy, bus franchises issued by the UK's largest Public Transport Executive (PTE), which is Transport for London (TfL), expect the franchisee to have functioning CCTV and alarm systems during all operational times (TfL 2017). Additionally recognised as important by Clarke and Smith was the removal of graffiti. Arguably, not only is this action aesthetically preferable but also it makes the mode of transport more pleasant to use and improves the reputation of the provider (TfL 2017).

Delbosc and Currie (2012) claimed that up to 10% of the population would use public transport more often if personal safety concerns were addressed (Crime Concern 2004 cited in Delbosc and Currie 2012:302). Their research asserted that some car drivers would switch to using public transport if it offered a similar level of personal safety to that of the car.

Delbosc and Currie measured the perceptions of trust which participants had in fellow travellers and the general socio-economic quality of transport and the community setting. Further variables of gender, location and distance from city centre and so on were then added. The study found that passenger gender, age and their trust in the provision of the public transport service were central to their decision to use it. This research, in tandem with the findings by Clarke and Smith (2000) above, reinforces the need for public transport providers to deliver safe and secure public transport, and this would improve the reputation of the operator and potential ridership.

Gardner, Cui, and Coiacetto (2017) contended moreover that public transport is a cornerstone of social life, especially in cities where car use is discouraged. They argued that the fear of being a victim of crime is one of the most important reasons that females choose not to use public transport or modifying their behaviour when they do use it. Gardner, Cui and Coiacetto recommend that solutions to this situation should include staff awareness training and their access to third-party reporting (TPR), which would obviate the necessity to report such a matter directly to a police officer. The research of Gardner et al. (2017) further underpins how victims could potentially experience hate crime and how this might also be assuaged by the introduction of staff training and third party reporting. However, this may be difficult to accomplish in a UK which, according to the findings of the EHRC (2011) report, is failing to protect females, children and transgender people from hate speech and hate acts in everyday society.

The rarity of research focusing specifically on hate crime taking place on public transport is noteworthy. However, one study by Purifoye (2015) examines racist hate acts on buses and asserted that public transport is similar to any social setting—except that it is more difficult to escape from its confines. Purifoye used participant observation in an ethnographic study to investigate the 'persistence of inequalities' which occurred in that environment (2015:288). Purifoye offered a theoretical framework to explain interactions between black and white people using buses. Whilst being polite, some interactions contained hidden nastiness originating from the white participant. Purifoye termed this concept 'nice-nastiness' (Purifoye 2015: inter alia). Aloofness by white passengers, argued Purifoye, implied that implicit racist behaviour was taking place. These behaviours included gazing through windows thus avoiding interaction with the black person sitting next to them, standing up rather than sitting next to a black passenger and whispered conversations rather than revealing to black passengers what they were saying (ibid., 2015). Purifoye argued that the white passengers were only using public transport at all because they have no transport alternative. In providing balance to this evidence, although these behaviours of nice-nastiness may well be as a result of a deeper-seated bias, there could be a range of explanations for such interactions. In other words, it is problematic to determine these behaviours strictly as racist. Many of us have been ignored whilst sharing crowded commuter trains. Perhaps some of the interactions cited in this research are merely private conversations between people who are acquainted. However, this remains an important, if rare, attempt at social observation in the public transport location.

1.9 Introduction Summary and the Structure of This Book

This introductory chapter has familiarised the reader with my motivation for researching disability hate crime on public transport in the UK and revealed the paucity of academic work which currently exists on this topic. The chapter has explored the definitions of hate crime and discussed particularities of disability hate crime. Definitions and models of disability were also discussed within this chapter, and this volume recognises its contentious use of the medical model of disability. A foray into crime on public transport was offered before the chapter specifically focused on the hate crime on public transport—albeit briefly. The importance that public transport plays in the lives of disabled people is worth stressing. Public transport cannot be overlooked in its role as an enabler for many people with disabilities. Without it, social isolation and limited access to public support, medicine and education could result. Therefore, it is important for the disabled passenger to be able to use public transport with safety and confidence and free of the fear of being abused.

The remainder of the book will take the reader on a journey within the research which inspired its publication. It will provide an explanation of the research methodology and its findings through to a discussion and recommendations for future safeguarding of disabled people on public transport in the UK. Chapter 2 will summarise how the research was accomplished and how it involved innovative methods of communicating with people with varying disabilities. This chapter will also discuss how approaches were made to public transport authorities and service providers to understand their methods for safeguarding passengers. Chapter 3 will capture and present the central evidence for this book, the experiences of victims and witnesses of disability hate crime on public transport. Not only will the immediate experiences be revealed but also any techniques of resilience and actions of collaboration between the abuser and allies. Chapter 4 explores the shorter- and longer-term impacts of the everyday abuse which people have faced. This chapter will reveal that victims' lives are changed inexorably because of seemingly low-level abuse and hostility. The chapter includes material which came to light from continuing contact with victims following the completion of the original research. Chapter 5 investigates the responses of the authorities and providers which have a legal duty to safeguard all passengers who use public transport. Chapter 6 will broadly discuss the research and findings whilst delineating an explanatory framework developed through the research to rationalise any collaboration which occurred during these attacks. It will align findings with established literature and examine future policy directions. Chapter 7 will conclude re-assessing the research journey, challenging existing epistemology and looking towards future research and aspirations. Having introduced the underlying research, therefore, the following chapter will detail how it was conducted.

Bibliography

Barnes, C., & Mercer, G. (2010). *Exploring Disability* (2nd ed.). Cambridge: Polity.

BBC (British Broadcasting Corporation). (1963). *Train Drives Itself*, BBC on this day 21/3/1963. London: BBC Online. Online at: http://news.bbc.co.uk/onthisday/hi/dates/stories/march/21/newsid_2546000/2546071.stm. Accessed 1 Mar 2018.

Beecroft, M., & Pangbourne, K. (2014). Future Prospects for Personal Security in Travel by Public Transport. *Transportation Planning and Technology, 38*(1), 131–148.

Bowling, B. (1999). *Violent Racism: Victimisation, Policing and Social Context.* New York: Oxford University Press.

Cameron, C. (2014a). The Medical Model. In C. Cameron (Ed.), *Disability Studies: A Students Guide.* London: Sage.

Cameron, C. (2014b). The Social Model. In C. Cameron (Ed.), *Disability Studies: A Students Guide.* London: Sage.

Chakraborti, N. (2015). *A Conversation Between the Author and Professor Neil Chakraborti 30/10/15.* Leicester: Department of Criminology, University of Leicester.

Chakraborti, N., Garland, J., & Hardy, S.-J. (2014). *The Leicester Hate Crime Project: Findings and Conclusions*. Leicester: University of Leicester.

Clarke, R., & Smith, M. (2000). Crime and Public Transport. *Crime and Justice, 27*(2000), 169–233.

College of Policing (CoP). (2014). *Hate Crime Operational Guidance*. Coventry: College of Policing.

Crime Concern. (2004). *People Perceptions of Personal Security and Their Concerns About Crime on Public Transport: Research Findings*. London: Department for Transport.

Delbosc, A., & Currie, G. (2011). Exploring the Relative Influences of Transport Disadvantage and Social Exclusion on Well-Being. *Transport Policy, 18*(4), 555–562.

Delbosc, A., & Currie, G. (2012). Modelling the Causes and Impacts of Personal Safety Perceptions on Public Transport Ridership. *Transport Policy, 24*(24), 302–309.

Equality and Human Rights Commission (EHRC). (2011). *Hidden in Plain Sight: Inquiry into Disability-Related Harassment*. Manchester: Equality and Human Rights Commission.

Equality and Human Rights Commission (EHRC). (2018). *How Is the UK Performing on Disability Rights? The UNs Recommendations for the UK*. Manchester: Equality and Human Rights Commission.

European Parliament. (2015). *Social Inclusion in EU Public Transport*. Brussels: The European Parliament.

Felson, M. (2002). *Crime and Everyday Life* (3rd ed.). Thousand Oaks: Sage.

Gardner, N., Cui, J., & Coiacetto, E. (2017). Harassment on Public Transport and Its Impacts on Women's Travel Behaviour. *Australian Planner, 54*(1), 8–15.

Hall, N. (2010). Law Enforcement and Hate Crime: Theoretical Perspectives on the Complexities of Policing Hatred. In N. Chakraborti (Ed.), *Hate Crime: Concepts, Policy, Future Directions* (pp. 149–168). Cullompton: Willan.

Her Majesties Inspectorate of Constabulary and Fire & Rescue Services (HMICFRS). (2018). *Understanding the Difference: The Initial Police Response to Hate Crime*. London: Her Majesties Inspectorate of Constabulary and Fire & Rescue Services.

Home Office. (2016). *Action Against Hate: The UK Government's Plan for Tackling Hate Crime*. London: Home Office.

Iganski, P. (2008a). *Hate Crime and the City*. Bristol: The Policy Press.

Iganski, P. (2008b). Criminal Law and the Routine Activity of 'Hate Crime'. *Liverpool Law Review, 29*(1), 1–17.

Iganski, P., & Lagou, S. (2015). The Personal Injuries of 'Hate Crime'. In N. Hall, A. Corb, & P. Giannasi (Eds.), *Routledge International Handbooks: Routledge International Handbook on Hate Crime* (pp. 34–46). New York: Routledge.

Independent Police Complaints Commission (IPCC) (Renamed Independent Office for Police Conduct (IOPC) 08/01/2018) (2011). *IPCC Report into the Contact Between Fiona Pilkington and Leicestershire Constabulary 2004–2007*. London: IPCC. Online at: https://www.ipcc.gov.uk/sites/default/files/Documents/investigation_commissioner_reports/pilkington_report_2_040511.pdf. Accessed 27 Oct 2018.

Jacobs, J., & Potter, K. (1997). Hate Crimes: A Critical Perspective. *Crime and Justice, 22*(1997), 1–50.

Mind. (2007). *Another Assault: Mind's Campaign for Equal Access to Justice for People with Mental Health Problems*. London: Mind.

Newton, A., & Ceccato, V. (2015). Theoretical Perspectives of Security and Safety in Transit Environments. In V. Ceccato & A. Newton (Eds.), *Safety and Security in Transit Environments*. Basingstoke: Palgrave Macmillan.

Papworth Trust. (2016). *Disability in the UK: Facts and Figures 2016*. Cambridge: The Papworth Trust.

Purifoye, G. (2015). Nice-Nastiness and Other Raced Social Interactions on Public Transport Systems. *City & Community, 14*(3), 286–310.

Rail Technology Magazine. (2017, March 7). Driver-only Trains and Safety: What's the Big Issue? London: *Rail Technology Magazine*. Online at: https://www.railway-technology.com/features/featuredriver-only-trains-and-safety-whats-the-big-issue-5769231/. Accessed 1 Feb 2018.

Reynald, D. (2010). Guardians on Guardianship: Factors Affecting the Willingness to Supervise, the Ability to Detect Potential Offenders, and the Willingness to Intervene. *Journal of Research in Crime and Delinquency, 47*(3), 358–390.

Sin, C. H. (2015). Hate Crime Against People with Disabilities. In N. Hall, A. Corb, & P. Giannasi (Eds.), *Routledge International Handbooks: Routledge International Handbook on Hate Crime* (pp. 193–206). New York: Routledge.

Sung-suk, V., Smith, M., & Ceccato, V. (2014). Commuters Using Public Transit in New York City: Using Area-Level Data to Identify Neighbourhoods with Vulnerable Riders (Safety on the Move). *Security Journal, 27*(2), 194–209.

Transport for London (TfL). (2017, August 14). *Interview Between the TfL Operational Standards Team Representative and the Author.*

Tripathi, K., Borrion, H., & Belur, J. (2017). Sexual Harassment of Students on Public Transport: An Exploratory Study in Lucknow, India. *Crime Prevention and Community Safety, 19*(3–4), 240–250.

CHAPTER 2

Revealing Incidents of Hate Crime on Public Transport: Working with Disabled People

Abstract This chapter helps the reader to understand to the process involved in collating the experiences of disabled people who have been victims of hostility. Ground-breaking methods were used to collect data from a group of people who, generally speaking, have been excluded from participating in such research. Interviews and focus groups were the mainstays of the author's study. Adaptive techniques were utilised to capture the thoughts of people with physical, mental and communication difficulties. Aside from victim data, data were additionally collected from the authorities who oversee UK public transport and the companies which provide it. Finally, the staff members who operate buses and trains were interviewed. These elements were incorporated to provide a rounded understanding of what is being done in the UK to safeguard disabled people from hostility on public transport services. Techniques of analysis, methodological reflection and areas which presented problems are also presented in this chapter.

Keywords Inclusivity • Victimisation • Research methods • Safeguarding • Participants

2.1 Chapter Introduction

From 2017 to 2019, I embarked on an impassioned research project, interviewing 56 victims and witnesses of disability hate crime on various modes of public transport in the UK. These people were drawn from an

D. Wilkin, *Disability Hate Crime*, Palgrave Hate Studies,
https://doi.org/10.1007/978-3-030-28726-9_2

original pool of 260 people who responded to my call for information. This work was ground-breaking as proportionately little research previously existed which was inclusive of disabled people themselves and none focusing on public transport hate crime as well. The study aimed to understand the nuances of such hostility and the long- and short-term impacts of abuse. Perceived *vulnerabilities* may have dissuaded previous researchers from asking pertinent questions of the very people who are at risk of this hostility (Goodley 1996). But with my experience of having been a victim of these crimes in my younger years, I wanted to find out more. I don't know whether it was a case of victim co-understanding or a brashness to uncover further victims of this abuse, but this mission managed to unearth some horrifying accounts. Moreover, understanding what happened to others who had been abused was not enough. Equality legislation exists in England and Wales to protect susceptible people. I needed to uncover the lengths to which public transport authorities and public transport service providers were going to safeguard their passengers from this abuse. To do this, I sought responses from 28 statutory authorities and 53 public service providers and interviewed members of public transport staff. This chapter is hopefully useful in explaining the methodology of the research underlying this monograph. The chapter will detail accessing research participants, the interviewing of participants and the adaptations made to fully enable participants, who have a range of disabilities, to contribute to it. The chapter will also outline the analysis of the research and how grounded theory was used within the study before critically reflecting the research approach.

2.2 Access to Research Sources

Any project involving human beings must be conducted with respect and dignity towards participants whilst offering them protection from any harm. Trust needs to be built between participants, and the researcher and participants need to know that they are an integral part of a research study and not just someone whose inputs are required. Goodley (1996) used the conceptual example of learning disabilities to reveal that people with disabilities are often excluded from research. Drawing similarities to prejudices which are applied to disabled people in their everyday lives, Goodley argued that there is a perception that people with disabilities have little to offer or are incapable of communicating effectively. Furthermore, there are examples of research exploring issues concerning disabled people whilst actually using non-disabled, proxy participants making a contribution in *lieu* of that from a disabled person (Cummins and Laraine Masters

2002). In other words, disabled people were being kept out of research, even if that research was centred upon their experiences. I argue that it would be irresponsible to ignore disabled people themselves. As the primary victims of hate acts are the focus of this book, these are the very people who need to be heard from. Furthermore, to ignore them would be to exclude up to 22% of the UK population (Scope 2018). The research for this book includes direct contributions from people with disabilities, their friends and carers to provide insightful knowledge about situations faced by disabled people, sometimes on a daily basis. For those who requested it, I also continued to update and involve participants as the research project developed, working together in a spirit of inclusivity and mutual support.

Regarding the collection of data, as Hollomotz (2018) argued, provided that adaptations are made, respect is given and flexible communications are used, there is no reason why disabled people should not fully contribute to research studies. Whilst social scientists might wish to avoid the ethical complexities of talking with disabled people, I took a different tack. In a similar approach to that used by Hardy (2017), I found that approaching people for a *chat* was often the best approach to initiate a research relationship. Later feedback informed me that this informal and friendly approach was felt to be less invasive than a more formal contact. Conversely, whilst formal approaches were made to UK-based Deaf and Disabled People's Organisations (DDPOs) for onward contact with established groups of disabled people, this strategy was mainly unsuccessful. Of the 66 organisations contacted only 6 responded, and then mainly unhelpfully. Whether they had a protective reticence towards exposing disabled people to a perceived risk or whether they could not allocate time to organising such contact is unknown. What is known is that a barrage of requests for donations followed from the DDPOs—but no help. Therefore, as a geographically limited, solo researcher with limited resources, I resorted to using social media and word-of-mouth communication to recruit participants.

I also contacted disability support groups locally to where I live, posted advertisements and spoke with voluntary organisations. Presentations concerning hate crime were given, and tea and cakes were tendered. Flyers were distributed, posters were posted and chats were initiated. My photograph was applied to posters and flyers, and this, according to feedback, increased the trustworthiness. The result of these personal interactions was that 56 people, either with a disability or associated with those having a disability, eventually contributed to the research. Social media was the most successful recruiting method with around 70% of participants being enlisted this way. More than just messaging, a bright campaign poster was applied to each social media posting. Both private messaging and public responses were encouraged. Away from social media, canvassing conducted locally to where I live was also successful but in a different and more personable way. The combination of these techniques brought forward responses from all over the UK. How the process of discussing disability hate crime with participants was handled is presented in subsequent sections.

2.3 Victim and Witness Participants

In total, 70 participants were involved in my study. Victim and witness interview participants contributed via semi-structured interviews, and these numbered 26. Those who contributed via focus group numbered 30. Further 14 public transport staff contributed via structured interviews. All victim participants were self-declared as having a disability or were witnesses to acts of hostility. Additionally, all participants, once informed of the definition of hate incidents and crimes in England and Wales, self-declared that they had been a victim of either a hate incident or a crime. Therefore, direct recruitment, self-declaration and self-recruitment meant that no *gatekeepers* were necessary to facilitate recruitment of contributors and this facet saved much time. All of the participants were given both a written and a verbal explanation of the research and how their inclusion was central to it. They were told that would have access to, but could not alter the published outcomes. If they latterly chose to withdraw from the study, they were assured that their data would be deleted. All participants were issued with a Helpsheet which I had produced as a further information source. This offered a contact list of support organisations which could be used if the participant required either for post-study information or for support. A complaints procedure through which a participant could raise criticisms of my research or my behaviour was added to the Helpsheet—although no complaints were made. Methods of contacting me were given including an email contact and a dedicated telephone line with a recording facility for out-of-hours communication. All participants underwent a mental capacity test (see the following section for more details) to protect the participant and ensure the viability of the informed consent which they had to freely give before taking part. Caregivers, guardians, friends or those appointed by the Court of Protection were also invited to be involved in discussing the informed consent process if desired by the participant. My interview technique was tested through pilot interviews which were conducted using two associates; also a pilot focus group was utilised. These events produced experiences which fed back into the live interviews. Techniques were honed, and questions were tweaked. These pilots were invaluable as a developmental intervention.

Anonymity of participants was facilitated by applying a numerical identifier to each contributor's transcribed data and to digital file names. Rudimentary metadata were collected to empirically record participant gender, age and the geographic location of the incident. All data were securely protected, and all potential risks were, as far as practicably possible, identified, mitigated against and documented in the ethical approval process. Whilst mitigating against the risk of harm to both the participants and myself, I also wanted to re-assure ethical approvers that every conceivable risk was being mitigated against to protect members of a group who had a proclivity to be perceived as being *vulnerable*.

2.4 The Interviews

Following recruitment, the primary method for gathering data from individual participants was via a telephone interview. A briefing note, stating the reason for the research, the purpose of participation and the rights of the participant, was emailed to each potential contributor. They responded to this by email, expressly giving their written informed consent to participate. This consent was re-requested verbally at the commencement of each interview when the mental capacity tests were also conducted. Such verbal consents were captured via audio recording which also captured the entire interview for later transcription. The 26 individual interviews that were conducted with victim or witness participants involved 14 females and 12 males. The telephone interview, with my telephone number withheld to reduce any risk of nuisance calls, was conducted at a time suitable to the participant. A different number was available for participants to contact me, and this used an answering service. A number of topics were covered during the course of each interview, and the questioning was adapted as revelations came to light. It was, I feel, also important that the participant was advised to find a suitably comfortable place for the interview. People with some disabilities need to be moved frequently, and this suggestion proved successful in preparing participants for up to one hour of conversation. It was also recommended that participants had a carer or friend with them if required. This carer or friend additionally had the proxy right to terminate the interview at any time as did the participant themselves—although carers could not, conversely, instigate informed consent to initiate the interview. Some interviews were hitherto unplanned and conducted with participants who were spontaneously recruited and wanted to contribute immediately. I did not want to lose any data and therefore respectfully accommodated these ad hoc participants.

Although the telephone interview does not allow for facial cues from the participants (Novick 2008), conversely, it does allow more privacy for the contributors and act as a *buffer* between the participant and the researcher should the participant feel exposed by the interview process (King and Horrocks 2010; Lechuga 2012). Moreover, response bias is reduced during telephone interviews because of the lack of facial cues. The technique was particularly appropriate for my study as the respondents were based all over the UK. I had scant resources to individually visit each participant, and therefore, an interaction which might have taken a few days to achieve could potentially be undertaken in only a couple of hours. Informed consent was obtained again, verbally, at the commencement of each interview, and the right to withdraw was repeated. To give respite needed because of upset or emotionality, pauses were taken where these were felt necessary or when requested.

2.5 Focus Groups

To triangulate data from interviews and provide a different setting and perspective, focus groups were also arranged. Focus groups are a valuable resource for this triangulation (King and Horrocks 2010). Five separate groups totalling 30 participants were undertaken with an average attendance of 6 contributors in each group. These involved 19 females, 9 males, 1 non-binary participant and 1 participant self-declared as intersex. Morgan proposes that 'most projects consist of 4-6 focus groups' after which 'little new data emerges' (Morgan 1996:144). Group members were drawn from existing support groups for disabled and deaf people; thus, group members were mainly already be acquainted with each other. This was intended to reduce the risk of unease amongst group participants. The original group leader remained in attendance throughout the sessions. Therefore, I had little control concerning participant recruitment and attendances regarding these focus groups—although all participants were within my target cohort. I facilitated the groups and gave an initial presentation focusing on disability hate crime before undertaking the discussion sessions. A similar interview guide was used for both the interviews and focus groups. Focus groups can lack the depth of meaning which can be gleaned from individual interviews (Cronin 2008), and the domination of some group members can reduce the value of the session (Morgan 1996). However, the focus group is a valuable method for gathering data enabling a blended conversation which allows for new themes to be introduced (Morgan 1996). Dominance or unfair behaviour was mediated by me, and I was grateful for being experienced as a facilitator. Informed consent protocols were conducted with as much privacy as was possible when the participants were entering the meeting place. The right to withdraw was reiterated during the session. Sessions were recorded and notated for later transcription. Often following these sessions, the conversation would continue regarding hate crime and associated topics. This was found to be a good opportunity to exchange contacts and interests. All participants, as with the interviews, were treated with respect and dignity, and their identities were anonymised.

2.6 Perceptions of Vulnerability and Adaptions

People with disabilities, especially learning difficulties and mental health issues, are often seen as too ***vulnerable*** to contribute to research (Goodley 1996). This perception of vulnerability might be invoked by risk-averse ethical overseers to restrict research from being undertaken. Researchers, of course, have a responsibility to protect all of their participants. To give assurance that participants are contributing freely, with the familiarity of the study, researchers need to know that their contributors are willingly giving their informed consent to participate. To ascertain that participants have sufficient mental capacity to give that consent, a test, which is widely used within the UK included by the Ministry of Justice, was utilised. The test is a two-stage mental capacity test, which is permissible under the Mental Capacity Act 2005 and was administered and guided by the Mental Capacity Act 2005: Code of Practice (updated 2016). This legislation is an enabling act. In other words: 'researchers should assume that a person has capacity, unless there is proof that they lack the capacity to make a specific decision' (Code of Practice, updated 2016:204). This legislation thus helps people to contribute to research—unless they specifically lack the capacity to do so. The test in the context of my study consisted of two questions: the first enquired if the participant had an impairing brain injury and the second asked if the participant could briefly describe the research aims. During interviews the test was conducted either over the telephone or in person, as required. During focus groups the test was conducted in as much privacy as was possible in a private area. No participant failed to reach the standard set by this test.

To be as inclusive as possible when gathering data from people with a wide range of disabilities, a number of adaptations were undertaken to reflect the needs of contributors. Examples of these were using face-to-face interviews in place of telephone interviews, where the participant wished for this and I could accommodate the request. Giving informed consent verbally, instead of in writing, was used in some cases. This was recorded and archived. The posting of briefing notes and informed consent requests through the physical mail system where email could not be used was also offered. Other more particularised adaptations were also made. An example was communicating via YouTube where one participant preferred a visual medium with follow-up questioning then conducted via email. Pictures were drawn by some participants when, for example, they had problems describing what had happened or when explaining the layout of the vehicle where the incident occurred. Video conferencing was also available but was not taken up. In two instances, a friend or carer received data from the participant and conveyed it to me over the telephone. During focus groups, role play occurred in some circumstances to describe situations and where visual enhancement was desired. Adaptations were mainly facilitated on the *spur of the moment* and in the stark realisation that if nothing was done to accommodate the participant, then valuable data could be lost. Emotional upsets during the discourse were dealt with by pausing or by reflecting on what should have happened. No participant withdrew, and six participants from both interview and focus group cohorts also agreed to take part in a thematic sampling panel (see below for further details).

2.7 Analysis and Theory Generation of Victim and Witness Data

To fully utilise participant data without losing any of its richness and meaning, the process of analysis needed to be just as robust as the process of collection. Recordings were transcribed and loaded into computer-assisted qualitative data analysis software (CAQDAS) where they were combined with written memoranda which captured emotionality and non-verbal responses. The chosen software was NVivo 11. Once within the software, the process of coding the material began with the first-level, open coding. Every incident and circumstance reported was coded separately to ensure that as many data as possible was captured. The first-level codes were then displaced by selective coding which was then utilised throughout the remainder of the analytical process. The open codes represented what the participant was saying at the *prima facie* level, what they found important to impart me. The selective codes moved on from that level to attach meaning to what the participants were saying. For example, an open code representing a verbal attack concerning the claiming of social benefits may latterly be changed to a selective code representing the concept of welfare resentment. In total, 109 selective codes were identified from the 56 victim participants involving 2246 selectively coded attributions. The general approach to coding and thematic construction was that used by Urquhart which I identified as being particularly useful to early stage researchers (Urquhart 2012).

Selective codes were latterly utilised to produce thematic relationships and ultimately to induce a grounded theory, thus enabling the germination of any explanatory frameworks which emerged from the data. Because of the paucity of previous research exploring the experiences of disability hate crime on public transport, there was little point in attempting to use established typologies or explanatory frameworks as presumptive sources. Moreover, because one component of my study was to consider the dynamics between victims, perpetrators and bystanders, the analysis needed to be flexible. Therefore, any adoption of previously established theory needed to be avoided, circumventing epistemological contamination when creating any fresh theorisation. As the selective codes were beginning to relate to one another, themes began to germinate. One dominant theme identified was where previously non-offending passengers were recruited by the principal offender to join in the abuse. Attempts of recruitment were reported in 71% of incidents on buses. In many of these cases, the newly recruited offenders then cooperated to abuse the disabled victim. This phenomenon will be explored in more detail in Chap. 6.

I was also mindful of the risk of researcher bias when conducting the analysis of data. This risk was mitigated against in the analysis phase by constant comparison between codes as they emerged and again following completion of the analysis. By making sure that codes carried the same meaning all the way through the analysis, consistency was applied and robustness was maintained. Codes were adjusted on numerous occasions to stabilise this creative process. Latter ratification of findings was undertaken through thematic sampling. This involved recruiting a panel of six participants, who had given particularly detailed accounts in the data collection phase, to analyse the findings. Their thoughts were collated, and suggested changes were used to refine the findings. The analysis of data from victims and witnesses will be explored and discussed in Chap. 6.

2.8 Intersectionality

Intersectionality theory asserts that when intersectionalities are involved, for example, by a victim being both disabled and gay, then victimisation is more likely to occur and is more likely to be amplified in effect by that intersectionality (for an example see Mason-Bish 2015). In my study, participants were asked on most occasions to identify their sexuality, faith and ethnic heritage so that metadata could be accrued to clarify any effect of intersectionality. Questions concerning this area were not asked in focus group settings to protect personal disclosures. The results of these questions put to the 26 interviewees reveal the following self-declarations. Faith: 8 participants declared as being Christian; 2 each represented the Hindu and Islamic faiths; 1 as Spiritualist and 5 did not associate with any faith. A further eight declined to respond. The ethnic origins of the participant cohort were declared as follows: 15 participants described themselves as white/British; 5 as British/Asian; 4 as white/Polish; 1 as white/American and 1 as white/Swedish. Metadata concerning sexuality revealed the following: 17 described themselves as straight; 2 as gay and 1 as transgender or intersex'. Six participants declined to respond. An overall picture of intersectionality was therefore difficult to draw as only a fractional sample of the 56 victim or witness participants answered these questions. Furthermore, very little intersectionality was revealed in my study. However, one couple, both black, did describe that being black and disabled needing to use wheelchairs did seem to make life worse. Furthermore, three participants mentioned that being gay or trans' may have added to their predicament. Conversely, one participant extolled his image as a gay wheelchair user of Asian origin as a focal point of his identity.

2.9 Public Transport Safeguarding Responsibility

As well as exploring the experiences of victims and witnesses, my research needed to establish what—if anything—had been accomplished to protect disabled and other passengers using public transport services. In the UK, either these services are regulated by a transit-specific *regulatory authority* or their operations are either overseen or influenced by a *local authority* which undertakes multiple municipal responsibilities. In many instances, services are also directly provided by these local authorities, for example, to transport children with learning difficulties. Local authorities may also provide services which would not be commercially viable on Sundays or during national holidays. Services directly provided by these authorities are often contracted out to private service providers.

The primary legislation in the UK concerning equalities, including those of disabled people, is the Equality Act 2010. Section 149 of the Equality Act creates the Public Sector Equality Duty (PSED). The PSED is clear that any agency or company conducting activities of a public nature, as defined under the Human Rights Act 1998, must adhere to the principles of the PSED. It applies to any public service procured and commissioned by any regulatory agency or local authority. The Equality Act, through its PSED, specifies statutory obligations to eliminate: discrimination, harassment, victimisation and other conduct prohibited by the Equality Act. Additionally, it stipulates a duty to advance equality of opportunity between persons who share relevant protected characteristics and those who do not and, moreover, to foster good relations between those groups. Therefore, the Equality Act not only specifies protective equality duties to be performed but additionally the promotion of behaviours and values which must be promulgated within all public sector activity in England and Wales. The Equality Act also demands that each authority publishes equality objectives and annual updates regarding how these measures are being met. The Equality and Human Rights Commission (EHRC) is responsible for oversight and enforcement of the Equality Act in the UK and consequently the PSED. The EHRC had reported that perceived vulnerabilities were causing disabled people not to receive the justice which they had a right to expect (EHRC 2011). The EHRC report also provided evidence that perceived vulnerabilities acted as triggers for abusers to victimise disabled people. The report additionally confirmed that public transport is a site of hate acts against disabled people. The UK Home Office (2016) hate crime action plan reinforces the view that public transport is a high-risk environment for hate crimes against disabled people and suggests some measures to tackle it; however, these mainly involve discussion groups and advertising campaigns (Home Office 2016). In a 2018 update to the 2016 action plan, the Home Office reinforced the centrality of the PSED to deliver public equality:

> *Public Sector Equality Duty*
>
> *The Home Office and the Ministry of Housing, Communities and Local Government, as public authorities, are bound by the Public Sector Equality Duty and therefore have due regard to the need to eliminate discrimination, harassment and victimisation, and foster good relations between persons who share a relevant protected characteristic and persons who do not share it.* (Home Office 2018:21)

As this section has illustrated, the legal position is clear. Any agency, regulator or authority conducting, or contracting out public service functions must not only practise the PSED and its values but also ensure that all of their contractors are applying it. In every aspect of the work of regulatory and local authorities, and in their influences over others, the PSED must be instilled and exercised. It is the PSED which provides equality assurance for disabled people and other protected groups.

2.10 Probing Public Transport Authorities and Providers

To ascertain if local and regulatory authorities were complying with their responsibilities to safeguard passengers, I raised 28 requests under the UK Freedom of Information Act 2000 (FOI) directed at those authorities. The authorities were selected on the basis that these were the areas in which my participants had suffered hostility. The FOI procedure obliges such organisations to respond candidly, within 20 working days, to public queries. A similar request was also sent to the UK Department for Transport. To determine if public transport providers were conducting themselves within the PSED, 53 requests for information were made to public transport service providers. The FOI could not be used for these requests unless the provider was a wholly owned subsidiary of a regulatory body or local authority—a situation which is relatively rare. Subsequently however, only six public transport providers responded.

The FOI requests to the authorities and regulatory bodies were raised as the following questions. These questions are being shown in full to reveal the exactitude and detail which was used. I did not want any of the recipients to argue that they had insufficient information upon which to make a response:

1. The Home Office strategy: Action Against Hate, 2016, indicates that public transport is a key area of concern for hate crimes being

conducted towards people with disabilities. What action is your organisation taking to reduce hostility and abuse against people with disabilities on your public transport services in your area?
2. Please send me your policies and strategies for dealing with the potential for hostility and abuse against people with disabilities on public transport services in your area.
3. What training interventions do you stipulate or suggest to enable public transport staff be aware of, and manage, the potential of hostility and abuse against people with disabilities on public transport services in your area?
4. How does your organisation raise awareness of the possibility of hostility and abuse against people with disabilities on public transport services in your area?
5. Please send to me your published equality objectives in relation to public transport provision in your area and clarify how you make these objectives accessible to the public.
6. Please send me any progress that you have made towards meeting equality objectives concerning public transport in your area.
7. Please clarify how you incorporate the Public Sector Equality Duty in your provision of public transport including when contracts are agreed with contracting service operators.

Most responses were received within the statutory time requirement. Some of the requests however were diverted to other agencies or companies which provide public transport. This action delivered a response only if that agency was itself obliged to respond to FOI requests. Otherwise, no response was forthcoming.

The 53 public transport providers which were contacted were asked:

> I am actively researching hostility against disabled people on all forms of public transport across the UK. I am looking for examples of how public transport providers strive to protect their customers.
>
> Would you be kind enough please to advise me if you have any policies in place or any training for your staff to recognise and manage hostility against disabled people on your services? Or, do you run any advertising campaigns aimed at raising awareness and protecting disabled travellers?

Furthermore, a structured interview was conducted with 14 current or recent members of public transport staff in the east of England. This approach was used to allow for speedy questioning when these staff had little spare time between performing their duties. Questions were posed concerning how much knowledge they had of disability equality requirements, their knowledge of disability hate crime and if they had received any training or advice to manage these abusive situations particularly those involving disabled people. It is noteworthy that all staff members questioned insisted on anonymity so that their employer was not aware that they had contributed. This anonymity was assured. The responses to requests to authorities and providers combined with the staff interviews and the resulting findings will be revealed and discussed in Chap. 6.

2.11 Research Problems

Finally for this chapter, it is important to emphasise, for future researchers, what worked in my research approach and what did not. Confidence in DDPOs was somewhat undermined by their reluctance to help. Not only did 60 of the 66 organisations contacted not help, they did not respond to my emails either. This I considered to be at the very least discourteous and unprofessional. Moreover, I was not expecting organisations which are founded to support people to maintain this degree of uncooperativeness. Naively perhaps, I considered that they would take every opportunity to explore, understand and alleviate the negative experiences of people that they are trusted to support. Of the six groups which did help with the research, they were excellent and could not have been more helpful. Additionally, I contacted politicians in the UK, across the political spectrum, who purported to support disabled people. The objective here was to receive support or advice. This approach was entirely fruitless. The only response, from a senior politician who claims to care for disabled people, was an application form to join their political party.

Another lesson learned concerned recruitment of participants. Social media, which was used for campaigning, could have been more widely used. Facebook and Twitter were my mainstays, however, on reflection, perhaps more participants could have been garnered by using more diverse social media platforms. Furthermore, in practical terms, the recording of focus groups also caused a problem. Because of the equipment, baggage or powerchairs used by individuals, the individual group members were often located some distance from the microphone. This resulted in a poor quality of the recording, and two sets of notes were additionally taken during each group discourse to reinforce data from the recordings and to make sure that no data were missed. During telephone interviews the hands-free loudspeaker was more useful than a telephone earpiece for some participants. This technique meant that contributors were not limited to having their arms in fixed positions for up to one hour of conversation. Requests by email to public transport service providers were often not responded to. Follow-up emails provided more pressure to respond but ultimately this entire approach produced little response. Finally, looking after the researcher is one facet which can easily be overlooked. Relaxation, reflection and perhaps even counselling may be necessary for any researcher involved in such potentially emotive work to allow them to recuperate following an upset. Besides learning from mistakes, good experiences can produce what might become best practice. Preparing telephone participants by advising them to find a comfortable place for up to one hour of conversation helped to shape expectations and no participant complained of fatigue. Carrying a mobile phone to focus groups was helpful for me when access to meeting places could not be affected. Having water on hand for focus groups and toilets nearby helped to avoid discomfort for both participants and researcher alike.

2.12 Summarising Chapter 2

This chapter has revealed the groundwork which was necessary to conduct my underlying research for this monograph. The chapter has described the access requirements which laid the ground for the interviews and focus groups that subsequently captured data from victims and witnesses to disability hate crime. How those interviews and groups were conducted was explained and issues of susceptibility were discussed. Adaptations were necessary for offering access to research for people with a range of disabilities. The subsequent section then dealt with the analysis of data. How data was captured from public transport authorities and service providers was outlined next. Finally, a reflection section offered a look back at some of the difficulties which arose and also the best practice which might be taken forward from my study. The chapter aimed to provide a route which other researchers might consider if they are researching people with disabilities. It also provided a toolbox of available resources, an example being the mental capacity test, which can be put into use in future research opportunities. Having discussed how the data was captured, Chap. 3 will offer the first tranche of data which is that from victims and witnesses of disability hate crime on public transport.

Bibliography

Cronin, A. (2008). Focus Groups. In N. Gilbert (Ed.), *Researching Social Life* (3rd ed.). London: Sage.

Cummins, R. A., & Laraine Masters, G. (2002). Proxy Responding for Subjective Well-Being: A Review. In *International Review of Research in Mental Retardation* (Vol. 25, pp. 183–207).

Equality and Human Rights Commission (EHRC). (2011). *Hidden in Plain Sight: Inquiry into Disability-Related Harassment*. Manchester: Equality and Human Rights Commission.

Goodley, D. (1996). Tales of Hidden Lives: A Critical Examination of Life History Research with People Who Have Learning Difficulties. *Disability & Society, 11*(3), 333–348.

Hardy, S.-J. (2017). *Everyday Multiculturalism and 'Hidden' Hate*. London: Palgrave Macmillan.

Hollomotz, A. (2018). Successful Interviews with People with Intellectual Disability. *Qualitative Research, 18*(2), 153–170.

Home Office. (2016). *Action Against Hate: The UK Government's Plan for Tackling Hate Crime*. London: Home Office.

Home Office. (2018). *Home Office: Hate Crime Statistics*. Online at: https://www.gov.uk/government/statistics/hate-crime-england-and-wales-2017-to-2018. Accessed 17 Oct 2018.

King, N., & Horrocks, C. (2010). *Interviews in Qualitative Research*. London: Sage.

Lechuga, V. (2012). Exploring Culture from a Distance: The Utility of Telephone Interviews in Qualitative Research. *International Journal of Qualitative Studies in Education, 25*(3), 251–268.

Mason-Bish, H. (2015). Beyond the Silo: Rethinking Hate Crime and Intersectionality. In N. Hall, A. Corb, & P. Giannasi (Eds.), *Routledge International Handbooks: Routledge International Handbook on Hate Crime* (pp. 24–33). New York: Routledge.

Mental Capacity Act. (2005). *Codes of Practice: Updated 2016*, (2016). London: The Stationery Office. Online at: https://www.gov.uk/government/publications/mental-capacity-act-code-of-practice. Accessed 27 Jan 2019.

Morgan, D. (1996). Focus Groups. *Annual Review of Sociology, 22*(1), 129–152.

Novick, G. (2008). Is There a Bias Against Telephone Interviews in Qualitative Research? *Research in Nursing & Health, 31*(4), 391–398.

Scope. (2018). *The Disability Perception Gap*. Online at: https://www.scope.org.uk/Scope/media/Documents/Publication%20Directory/Disability-Perception-Gap-report-FINAL.pdf?ext=.pdf. Accessed 29 Nov 2018.

Urquhart, C. (2012). *Grounded Theory for Qualitative Research: A Practical Guide*. London: Sage.

CHAPTER 3

Everyday Experiences of Victimisation Against Disabled People

Abstract The core of the data from the victims of disability hate offences and hostility are presented within this chapter. Techniques of abuse are revealed along with the immediate reactions of the victims. What becomes clear in this chapter is the exhaustion which victims suffer preventing them from engaging with the abuser and wanting to flee the scene. The everyday nature of the abuse becomes evident. Not only is there simply no point in retaliating to these events, but often there is little point in reporting these incidents either. Successful responses to reporting are rare. The reaction of fellow passengers when abuse occurs is of interest. Often onlookers ignore the obvious plight of the victim. Moreover, in many cases, fellow passengers are known to collaborate in the abuse. How staff manage these incidents may be crucial. The attitude and actions of staff members during these incidents are also brought to light.

Keywords Techniques of abuse • Everyday abuse • Exhaustion • Reporting • Onlookers • Collaboration

3.1 Chapter Introduction and Metadata

The data which I gathered relating to disability hate crime on public transport in the UK were rich, detailed, sometimes startling and almost always distressing. This chapter will explore the qualitative data gathered from

D. Wilkin, *Disability Hate Crime*, Palgrave Hate Studies,
https://doi.org/10.1007/978-3-030-28726-9_3

victims and witnesses which illustrated the ongoing hostility faced by disabled people using public transport in the UK. Interviews and focus groups were conducted and then transcribed. Open coding was used and then developed into selective codes within the computer-assisted qualitative data analysis software. Latterly, themes were drawn from the coding. Grounded theory was used to capture emergent themes and explanatory frameworks.

Although a qualitative study, an outline of metadata may be useful. Such was the abundance of material that 109 selective codes were generated from within the 2246 coded attributions drawn from these data. Study participants had self-declared as both having a disability and as were having been victims of hate crimes or incidents. The cohort consisted of the 56 victim and witness participants, involving 33 females and 21 males. The range of disabilities among the cohort included learning difficulties, mental health issues, physical impairment and communications difficulties. Co-morbidity existed with some participants. Abuse was conducted mainly aboard buses and trams or at bus or tram interchanges (74%) with trains and Tubes[1]—or their interchanges—being cited in 21% of incidents. The other significant mode of transport was the taxi, where 3% of incidents occurred. Other offences ensued when using public on-demand bus systems (e.g., Dial-a-Ride bus services), on ferries and when using public-hire bicycles. When hate incidents and crimes were legally defined for participants, 72% declared that they had been a victim of a hate crime and 27% of a hate incident. Data concerning the abusers reveals that: 50% were male; 84% were white and the age range was 14–70 with an approximated median age of 25.

Participants declared as having suffered violence in 45% of incidents. This violence in its physical form often consisted of jostling, pushing and being prevented from occupying priority spaces and seating. In non-physical forms, violence was cited as being expressed through threatening language, psychological abuse and abusive verbal attacks. In the overwhelming number of incidents (85%), the victims felt that they were unwilling or unable to retaliate during incidents. Many contributors had declared exhaustion as being the main reason for not being able to react to their abuser. Long-term impact resulted from 70% of attacks, with this effect often enduring for months or years following the incident. A loss of

[1] The Tube was a colloquial term and is now accepted branding for the London Underground transit mode operated by Transport for London.

confidence was experienced by 67% of the cohort which often resulted in a reluctance to use public transport in the future. Of these participants, 48% changed their lifestyles to avoid future incidents, and 51% of these people felt socially isolated because of these lifestyle changes. Long-term and lifestyle impacts are a facet that will be explored further in Chap. 4. Victims and witnesses also expressed that they occasionally tried to engage staff to intervene during incidents. Although staff positively helped in 2% of incidents, the vast majority (84%) were worryingly met with indifference, ignorance or an inability to help. Furthermore, in 8% of occurrences, staff members were themselves the abusers, acting either alone or in consort with others. Victims and witnesses reported these incidents of hostility in 28% of the incidents, of which 30% were followed up but only 8% of which resulted in outcomes considered successful by the participant.

The behaviour of fellow passengers during incidents is of interest. Fellow passengers overwhelmingly ignored these abusive situations even when what was happening was seemingly obvious. Indeed, help was given in support of the disabled victim in only 4% of incidents. Arguably of greater concern were the occasions where fellow passengers were willing to assist the principal offender. On 71% of occasions on buses and trams and on 23% of occasions on trains and Tubes, formerly non-offending passengers joined in the abuse against the victims, allying themselves with the initial abuser. This facet will be explored further in Chap. 6.

Having outlined the quantitative data, the remainder of this chapter will focus on the qualitative responses to the study, and this forms the bulk of experiences from participants. It will reveal the experiences of abuse and the impacts of that abuse. The following sections will convey: techniques of abuse, the immediate impact, the victims' immediate responses to hostility and any techniques of resilience or retaliation employed by the victim. Experiences of collaboration between the principal offender and other passengers are also examined as are the actions taken by staff either at the scene or later when incidents were reported. Content will be supported by direct citations from those involved, and these are identified in *italics*. The identities of participants will however remain anonymous.

3.2 Techniques of Abuse

The data revealed that the techniques of abuse used against victims are seemingly either active or passive. Passive abuse is characterised as those where abusers often used jibes or *banter*. Other passive abuses might include occupying a larger area of a seat so that a disabled person is unable to occupy it or being reluctant to allow access to priority areas. One of the most prevalent passive abuses is avoiding the disabled person's obvious plight or pleas for assistance; this evasion has a similar result to being actively abused in that the victim feels unsupported and alone (Garcia 2018). Some examples of passive abuse follow:

> *He looked at me and started dribbling. He had clearly seen me dribble, but I can't help myself. He winked at me. He knew what he was doing. He was making me feel like a psycho.*
>
> *I asked if anyone could help me to get to the door—I have never seen so many heads turn toward windows. It was like synchronised swimmers all acting at once. I wouldn't have said that this a hate incident but someone said 'they get paid enough [referring to welfare benefits], they can stand'.*
>
> *I politely asked for the seat and was told 'cripples at the back'.*

Conversely, active abuse includes instances of name-calling, swearing or expressing that the disabled person is of a lower social value. Threatening and also actioning violence against the victim were more extreme actions. Assistance, when requested, was brazenly withheld by the abusers. The abuser might additionally notify the victim that any help is being denied and this worsened the feeling of isolation for the victim. Participants spoke of blocked aisles, seats with items placed to prevent use, being jostled and priority seats and spaces being withheld from those who needed them. Many participants reported that this was a normal journey expectation for them. These are examples of active abuse from bus travel:

> *He moved to the middle of the seat, I asked him to move and he completely ignored me. I asked again and he opened his legs to prevent me sitting there and called me a scrounger. Why, what have I done to upset him?*
>
> ...
>
> *A guy shouted from the back of the bus that 'I smell of shit and should be thrown off the bus'.*
>
> *I couldn't believe it; he unfolded my wheelchair in the bay and threw it off of the bus. I was trapped and humiliated. I was totally isolated. The driver got it back for me. But I felt so vulnerable, alone, fucking low and shit.*
>
> *One female was waiting for a ramp to be deployed to alight from a train. The platform staff members were not there to meet her.*
>
> *They [the fellow passengers] were like a pack of wolves. A woman said that if they [the staff] didn't arrive soon they should just push me off. She said that we [disabled people] were always looking for preferential treatment. They [the other passengers] were baying at me thinking it was a great idea.*

Another female victim was boarding a rural train. Visibly impaired and needing to use two sticks. The difficulty that she was having was seemingly obvious, yet:

> *They let their dogs growl at me and jump up at me. I said 'please control your dogs' and they said 'they're only having fun, they won't hurt you'; you could throw your stick [walking stick] for them [laughter]. But they were hurting me, my heart was pounding I was so scared. The next train was an hour away and so I couldn't get off.*

Much resentment at the possibility that disabled people might receive enhanced benefits and privileges or that they might possess an expectation to occupy privileged spaces in public transport vehicles was evident—whether or not this was true. Much of this resentment was perceived when disabled victims needed extra room or when they had mannerisms which may have resulted in other passengers needing to adjust their seating position or behaviour:

> *Every day, twice a day, I used the tram. My friend, my carer, my so-called friend… was the very person who reduced me to uselessness. She told everyone how much benefit I got, how filthy I was to clean and how she never got any sleep. I always looked at the floor because others were judging me. When she died it set me free …*
>
> *He asked me how many people he was paying to wash my arse.*
>
> *I was told that I could put my sticks away now that I had signed-on [enrolled for provision of state benefits]; I didn't need them until the next time.*

On other occasions seemingly innocent comments from some people can cause just as much offence as deliberate ones; 17% of participants reported these occurrences. Some of these were difficult to declare as hate-related incidents or crimes because of the difficulty in determining abuser intent. A female, wheelchair user who had a baby with her was asked:

> *How could you [a person in a wheelchair] have a baby? Surely you can't look after it? You should have it taken away [by the state authorities].*

Some fellow passengers make explicit accusations that the disabled victim was to blame for delays to public transport. Participants voiced how they are targeted after they had boarded already delayed services. Some of these reported that they feared the bus or train being delayed because this increased the risk of them being labelled as scapegoats for passenger frustrations. Participants were made to feel that the situation was their fault:

Three of them started on me. All sorts of stuff like: 'we were all right 'till you got on' and 'I'm going to be late because of you'. Another idiot joined-in and said 'they should have special services for them flids, they're not to blame and we should feel sorry for them really'.

The driver was helping me on and making a big deal of it. He then announced to the rest of the bus that 'sorry about the delay, it's because of him'. I thought you cheeky bastard, but what could I say?

Occupancy of seats and priority areas triggered many problems, especially in the bus environment. Numerous incidents involved buggies and prams parked in wheelchair bays. Asking to use these areas often caused consternation and conflict. Victims felt devalued because fellow passengers did not understand, or did not want to understand, the needs of the disabled person and/or refused to vacate the area. A male participant with fibromyalgia which resulted in uncontrollable weight gain tried to occupy a priority seat on a train and was stopped from doing so and told:

You would take up three seats you fat cunt.

One wheelchair-using female asked for pram and a suitcase to be removed from the wheelchair bay. Her pleas were ignored so she started to remove them herself. The reaction was:

She [the pram owner] screamed at me, hysterically. She said 'you spacco bastard you want to eat my baby' she turned to the rest of the bus and said: 'they [disabled people] eat babies; they should be locked-up'. Why would I want to eat a baby?

Other examples:

I said please could you move your pram. She said 'my baby's asleep'. I said that I understood but if you wouldn't mind because I need to be on this bus to get to work, I have no alternative. She said 'my baby's asleep'. I had enough; I said look, I need to use this space. She then told the driver that I was an evil disabled bitch because I was trying to wake her baby.

I asked her to move her pram, I was really nice. She just stood there and said 'no' and looked at her phone. The driver asked her to move or to fold the pram up. All we got was 'no'. She then sighed, looked up and said 'why weren't you just killed at birth'. I collapsed; I was stunned, I died inside. Am I that worthless? …

Jibes and *banter* have the potential to quickly develop into more abusive situations. An example follows where jibes from a group of young males, which may have been initiated in misplaced humour, soon became personally and violently abusive towards a wheelchair-using female on a train:

> *They sang to me: 'skid the flid, skid the flid', over and over. They were threatening to push me along the road, my God was I terrified.*

People with obvious mannerisms were targeted. One female participant with Tourette's syndrome which resulted in her banging her chest with her fist when she has a tic and who is also a wheelchair user was targeted:

> *The bus smells of shit since you got in; you've got shit on your bum because you are disabled.*
>
> ...
>
> *Bang harder on your chest so that you have a heart attack and end up in a coffin ...*

Participants also suffered physical violence. One female participant, who was using a wheelchair and travelling by train, experienced the following. A crowd of football followers surrounded the participant, and:

> ... *I could feel something behind me. Then one said 'stop wanking over her'. I shouted for help but nobody could hear me. They were laughing by then.*

In another extreme case the driver of the bus was one of the instigators of violence against one female participant who has a daughter who uses a wheelchair with learning difficulties:

> *He said that prams should have priority and we were a pain because we were so useless. We had a meeting with the manager at the bus garage because of all the abuse we were getting and the staff didn't help. But I knew that he told his drivers that babies in prams were more important than 'spacco's in wheelchairs'.*

Some victims have had their photographs taken without their consent which were later posted on social media with defamatory comments alongside. This might arguably be seen as an attempt to incite virtual collaboration via social media.

There it was, on Facebook—me as a paedophile? I know they were targeting me because I'm disabled, they told me that before ....

This section has revealed some of the many of the abuses which were imparted by participants to my study. The reader needs to be aware, however, that these were only a representative sample of all of the comments made. The space within this monograph is limited, and therefore, only a proportion of each type of comment can be represented here.

3.3 The Immediate Impact on the Victim

Almost all of the participants stated that they found that abuse on public transport makes them feel humiliated, embarrassed and intimidated in the immediate aftermath of a hate crime or incident. Many contributors stated that in the immediate aftermath, they felt like abandoning using public transport in the future, indicating that they would rather walk than use public transport because of the abuse they suffer. Of this group many victims complained about feeling like a *freak*, being centre stage in a public arena and having to cope without help or support in humiliating situations. Typical examples follow:

... the other passengers were laughing by now and I was just the fool – and a gay fool at that.

... people laugh at me; they don't do it until I say something. Some kids call me the 'helium woman'.

It is revolting how people treated you. Everyone has little accidents ...

... the [female] driver leaned out of her cab and said 'you lot of stiffs are a fucking nuisance'.

... '[the] stinking bastard has shit himself'. This got laughs from some. Then one joined-in and said 'dirty fat bastard' and his partner said 'we're all going to throw-up because of him'.

Humiliation and intimidation often worsened because the victim was unable to move away from the abuser, often because they were limited to using a priority space or unable to physically move. Participants also expressed feelings of weakness and powerlessness before, during and after bouts of abuse. They reported already feeling physically weak after propelling their wheelchair onto the bus and needing to find a secure position within the vehicle. But subsequent abuse then exhausted them further. Some examples follow:

... I have pain all the time I haven't got the energy to complain!

The [male] bus driver literally ignored my request to lower the bus ramp. He didn't even acknowledge my presence.

I had another incident where kids were photographing me using their phone. I was powerless to stop them.

We couldn't shift the victim. We had to call an ambulance she just seemed to have melted on to the floor. I was really shocked at that.

Victims feeling different and that their values had been attacked were also common experiences:

... these people should think that I should not have been born—sometimes I wish I had not been.

One woman who couldn't find room for her pram, she told me that I should 'die soon and to make room for the living'.

3.4 Victim Acceptance, Resilience and Retaliation

Victim's immediate responses when confronted by an abusive situation varied. Most were passive, non-retaliatory actions. Actions taken by the victim were often verbal or facial expressions. However, the most utilised immediate action adopted by victims was just to accept the situation. One male participant, accompanying his wheelchair-using wife, was spat at whilst at a bus station:

I felt the need to defend my wife. It affects me if she is insulted ... we both feel it. She had to sit there and clean off the spit. I had to watch her being humiliated. She cried. I felt so useless because for not retaliating I did nothing about it. I feel that my wife supports me more than I support her.

Further comments of being unable to retaliate included:

... dumbfounded.

... I was in disbelief.

...I really felt shocked!

... I never knew that people would be so callous.

... I felt physically sick.

... all of my dignity went away.

Participants who utilised coping strategies or accepted the situation revealed that they had little support from others; they often felt alone and powerless in facing abuse. Examples were noted where the participant moved to another location within the vehicle or alighted altogether to avoid further hostility or conflict. However, they indicated that alighting from public transport caused its own problems. There may be a lengthy delay between services, or the service may be unreliable. Contributors asserted that they should not have to alight because they were the victim of someone else's abuse. The impact of staff behaviours on victims is also important. Participants felt that a staff member could potentially greatly help in an abusive situation—albeit they could also make it worse.

Victims were not always passive in their responses to abuse however. Whilst some victims remain shocked by abusive experiences, some victims do retaliate. Many victims have adopted coping mechanisms. However, these retaliations were recorded in only a small number of incidents. Whilst two participants in the cohort paradoxically, actively agreed with their abusers, many also tried to reason with the offender; here is one example:

> *The lady in the chair said 'I have been waiting here for half an hour and I don't deserve to be treated with such disrespect. Sort this problem out or I'll find someone who will'.*

A favoured method of coping with abuse was to practise self-control, to:

> *... pick myself up ...*

Or to:

> *... bite my tongue ...*

Whilst others used retaliatory tactics to overcome the abuse:

> *... I can see you looking at me like I'm a freak. I know who you are and how jealous you are [of me].*

Other participants favoured a more robust approach:

> *... they are always loud always provoking you everything is 'f'In' and 'c...' they want you to be notice ... Makes them look good. If you bang into them they think hang on a minute this old boy might give me some ...*

Acceptance of the victim's plight occurred in most occasions. In a few instances participants found that onlookers were positively helpful in managing their situation, although this mainly consisted of helping the victim to re-position their wheelchair or equipment, or finding somewhere else to sit.

Some participants readily offered solutions and suggestions towards combatting hate crimes and incidents on public transport in the future. Focus groups frequently discussed the possibility of allocating separate bays for both wheelchair users and for buggies on buses and in trains. However, the majority of participants were ultimately against this proposition. They considered that sufficient bays and regulations were in place already, but as these were not being enforced, there was little point in having more. One solution put forward by a participant who was a citizen of the Republic of Ireland was to charge a fee for unfolded prams and buggies, an approach which seemed to work well in the Republic. An alternative is to provide storage space only for folded-up buggies. This participant believed that the size of the buggy is reflective of the desired status of the person pushing it. Therefore to have only space for folded buggies would render this status invisible and thus remove the necessity to characterise it. Other participants suggested that sentencing needs to be enhanced for convicted perpetrators of hate crime and in particular disability hate crime. Contributions more broadly revealed that education was the key to helping the general public understand the plight of disabled people generally and in particular when using public transport. Examples of raising awareness through education included: an understanding of assistance dogs; understanding disability rights issues; an awareness of access issues and the practical, physical and psychological problems which disabled people face in their daily lives. One participant made it clear that he does not want to promote that disabled people should stop using public transport. This participant wants public transport to be used more widely to protect services—a point that attracted wide agreement in that focus group. He additionally feels that it is disabled victims who also need awareness training:

> *I know that restricted growth people try to avoid using public transport – although experiences are rare. … I do not want to deter anyone from using public transport at all. We should learn how to use it together and get on together to do it.*

An overwhelming number of participants thought that staff needed to be aware of disability and equality issues and receive appropriate training regarding hostility against disabled people. Furthermore, staff need to be made aware of how to and where to report crimes and incidents. Staff members need to know, and have the confidence in, reporting these incidents without any prompting or requests from passengers. They also need to have access to third-party reporting (TPR) avenues. This would mean that they need not spend extended periods of time reporting matters to the police. Such an action would save time for the employees; after all, staff absent from the workplace may result in service cancellations. Some comments from participants of staff behaviour follow:

> *… it was not necessarily the fault of the drivers … they should receive proper training.*
>
> …
>
> *You shouldn't have to ask – it's not a failure of the individual bus drivers, it's a failure of company management.*
>
> *Tell them [the staff] that we have feelings, that we are human. I don't want the weight of the law to be on anyone… I just want people to be aware of each other's' needs and to be respectful of that. Nothing heavy!*
>
> *… I think training for drivers and transport staff on hate crime and ways to respond and show care to people affected by it would be useful.*
>
> *… When I have got to know drivers they are more confident in knowing what I need and respond to that they are more confident in what they do. …. That familiarity really helps! I was chatting to a driver and she said that she asked a buggy user to apply the rules and she was told not to apply the regulations as this can lead to a complaint and they don't want complaints.*

3.5 Passengers Collaborating to Abuse

Some incidents of abuse entailed the principal offender recruiting formerly inoffensive fellow passengers who then collaborated in abusing the victim. Participants reported this phenomenon in 71% of incidents on buses and trams and also in 23% of incidents on trains, with 52% of participants experiencing this effect overall. Collaborative Alienation, as I have labelled the phenomenon, involved a range of recruitment techniques performed by the principal offender, including the use of humour and justification practices for the actions used. Techniques of recruitment were not consistently successful. The reaction of the formerly unoffending passengers followed one of three paths: successful recruitment, where the new associates allied themselves with the principal offender; oppositional, where sympathy was shown towards the victim; or finally, ignorance of the victimisation. The latter was accomplished, for example, by averting gaze or by focusing on a newspaper. The following example is one of many where the principal offender loudly verbalises the abuse and justifies the offending. In this example a victim tries to access a wheelchair bay, and the offender, in denying access because her baby was asleep, looks towards fellow passengers for support:

> *... she just looked straight ahead and said nothing. I tackled her and said ... you would make me wait for the next bus just in case you might wake your baby? She then started screaming at me ... calling me a parasite [abuse] blaming me for living on benefits [justification]. She was not talking to me though, but to others. I was in tears and everybody was looking at me. I was in the middle of the aisle and I was crying*
>
> ...
>
> *The mother was still ranting about being 'a fucking nuisance'. Most others seemed to have some sympathy with me though.*
>
> ...
>
> *... [However] another male passenger did say that 'I should be ashamed of myself'. She [the principal offender] was looking around at the other passengers on the bus and still she was calling me a parasite and telling people that I was living on the dole. She wished for everyone to know that I was a 'sponger'.*

Further examples of recruitment included similar justification techniques. A female powerchair-using participant had an attack of depression and anxiety on a train journey. Some of the other passengers began an engagement to encourage her to alight from the train before a wheelchair ramp had arrived:

> *I was telling all the other passengers that I couldn't go anywhere until I got help to alight. I was trying to explain my situation. Then a man came along, he was looking out of the train for me and said that nobody was coming to help.*
>
> ...
>
> *Then another man loudly said to anyone who could hear 'we can't wait here forever'.*
>
> ...
>
> *... another guy came up and said that I was making everybody late—he was saying this so loudly and looking for support so that everyone would blame me.*
>
> ...
>
> *That was followed by cheers and yells from other passengers. This arrogant woman in a very expensive and tailored suit said that they should 'tip me on to the platform'. There was more laughing. I was so scared.*
>
> ...

Devaluing the disabled passenger as a *freak*, or using equally distressing language, was commonly used. This involved highlighting the *difference* of the disabled passenger and making supplementary derogatory remarks. Mannerisms including facial differences and walking disabilities were often used to highlight these differences:

> *I had been shopping and feeling so tired because the lifts didn't work. I had to ask others to help, which is embarrassing anyway. Then this guy started telling the other bus passengers that disabled people are a joke and that we are useless and 'get in the fucking way'. The others started laughing and that's when it got really scary. He said 'they take-up room, stink, wipe their shit everywhere and cost us money …'*
>
> …
>
> *He walked off but was smiling and taking appreciation from his audience. I know that was blocking the aisle, I didn't want to be there. He was saying that 'if there were a fire we would all be dead and I would be a murderer'. Someone else then said that I was selfish and dangerous.*
>
> *He said 'keep away from the twitcher, you might catch something'.*

One example of labelling a disabled passenger as a nuisance was used by a female bus driver:

> *I was moving toward [getting on] the bus but the ramp was still not lowered. The door was open so I asked if she would lower the ramp. She turned to me and told me that I was a 'fucking nuisance'—she did it quietly so that other passengers would not hear this. But then she turned to those passengers and said, quite clearly 'she's got to come on. It will slow us right down but don't blame me blame her'. I was being made a freak. Others laughed; some were patient and looked sympathetic. But one bloke said to his mate that 'we're all fucked now'. Do you know how I felt? Do you know what that feels like?*

A male victim revealed:

> *Then he turned to the other passengers and said 'they should have special buses really shouldn't they?'*

Passengers signified their alliance with the principal offender in many ways; examples of this were smiling, nodding, laughing or signalling approval through supportive comments. It was somewhat difficult to establish when conditions were considered favourable by allies to commence collaboration. However, five participants verified that recruited allies seem to wait until it appears safe to do so before joining the abuse:

> *I've seen this happen on more than one occasion; the main bloke, the one who starts it, looks around for support. If it seems that the main bloke is doing quite well, then others join-in. once a few start then it's a free-for-all. It's as if they feel that they can operate in safety, without blame. It's like it all comes out, all of their frustrations at once.*

The same participant thought that these allies were also trying to protect themselves from being the next potential target:

> *It's like a comedy show, you know, if you don't join-in your next. Nobody wants to be picked-on so, sorry, but you're going to get it from me as well.*

An alternative outcome to abusing the victim by the potential recruit was the avoidance of the ongoing victimisation. On many occasions onlooker ignorance followed abuse and attempted recruiting by the principal abuser. Whilst not directly abusive perhaps, acts of ignorance can leave the victim feeling isolated and devalued. This example is from a female bus passenger:

> *For ten long minutes everyone on the lower deck listened to a public shaming of my body my life and my worth. And then it followed, the total silence that left me more exposed and isolated than any of the vitriol that had been directed at me. I desperately needed someone on that bus to acknowledge what had taken place – that didn't happen.*
>
> …
>
> *On the bus I felt incapacitated, in part, by the inaction of my fellow passengers*
>
> …
>
> *I didn't need them to know exactly what to do to help. But I did want them to be present and to acknowledge what was happening to me.*
>
> …
>
> *No one else spoke at all; there must have been 20 people downstairs on the bus.*
>
> *Do you know it's funny. They find something in the newspaper which they had not seen before. Something so fascinating that they must read it at that moment.*

On some occasions public sympathy did result from a principal offender attempting to recruit formerly unoffending passengers to help with an abusive attack. My study however noted very few instances where sympathy resulted. Here is one example:

> *A couple of people looked sympathetic but the rest looked away.*

Some collaborators used camera-equipped mobile phones to record images. Two of these were found published on social media alongside derogatory comments concerning the disabled victim and supporting the act of abuse. This perhaps introduces a more subtle and covert form of collaboration where any potential direct conflict can be avoided. Rather this can be embarked upon later, from a place of covert seclusion where online abuse can be promulgated and the identity of the abuser concealed. This section has revealed that not only might victims be wary of future abuse from a single offender but also from groups of allied abusers. Collaborative Alienation is a theory which will be expanded in Chap. 6.

3.6 Actions Taken by Staff and the Reporting of Incidents

Members of staff can arguably make a journey more pleasant or add to passenger frustrations. Both positive and negative responses shown by staff during or following incidents of hostility were captured in my research. Most of these data refer to incidents occurring on buses. In this section many incidents were noted. Staff positively assisted in 13% of incidents. On two occasions (1%) the bus driver physically removed an offender from the bus. This is one example:

> *Then he took a swing at me. I said son that will be the biggest mistake that you have ever made … and then the driver got out and pushed him off the bus. Good lad!*
>
> *On a number of occasions the bus driver intervened to make the offender aware of the distress which they were causing:*
>
> *… the bus driver noticed it and he was the one that stepped in and told them to mind their language in a nice way.*
>
> *I did ask a driver to obtain the priority seat for me because this old biddy refused to move and he did that for me.*
>
> …
>
> *He got out of his cab and asked the old dear to move. She refused, and loudly said she was there first and blind people get special buses and I should be on one*

of those. The driver was great. He said well I'm not moving until you move. So she did. You couldn't make it up!

However, the greatest number of examples in this category illustrated that the staff member took little or no action to intervene. In 78% of incidents the member of staff did not do anything to protect the disabled, or any other, passenger. In most of these cases participants noted that they did not seem confident of what to do to help the victim. There are numerous examples which exemplify this unwillingness:

> *One lady was told to piss off because she asked to use the priority seat. My member reported this to the driver who said that he had no authority to do anything about it.*
>
> *The bus driver did not know what to do nor had any idea of priority. He didn't really want to get involved really.*

On some occasions where staff members were asked to get involved, they revealed why they were unwilling or ill-prepared to assist. Many cited their lack of awareness of what to do or what their responsibilities were when questioned by the victim. The following examples illustrate:

> *I then asked the driver to sort out this situation but he said "there's nothing that I can do". I said well I cannot just sit here in the aisle and he said well you might have to get off the bus then.*
>
> *The driver, the usual scenario, would not do anything, did not move, and just did nothing at all. Sometime later, a woman with a pram, I had my headphones on, she wanted to get on the bus. I tuned-in a bit and a scene was unfolding. She was told she could not get on the bus because a wheelchair was in the bay. The driver was wrong; He should have suggested that she fold it up. That makes our lives as wheelchair users harder because he didn't offer her the chance to fold her buggy.*
>
> *The driver said to me 'what do you want me to do about it love. You're on here for free you might as well put up with it'.*
>
> *When I was having the seizures whilst doing my degree I had a seizure on the 83 bus to a posh area. I had woken up back to consciousness and I was the black slimly built bus driver pacing up and down looking really anxious. But what upset me was that he had shown no concern at all. I would have sat with the person or got assistance. It was just that nobody had the sense to sit with that person and wait for assistance.*

On a very few occasions the disabled victim or associate did question the staff member as to why they were refusing to help when the questioner was clearly a victim of abuse from another passenger. Some examples of staff responses follow:

> *'What do you want me to do? Tackle him to the floor? I have enough to worry about taking money and putting up with nutters on the road without having to babysit you'.*
>
> *'I can't help—I don't honestly know how to help. What do you want me to do'?*
>
> *'I'm not allowed to leave my cab'.*
>
> *'Who do you think I am, Superman'? He laughed at turned to the passengers and just shook his head.*
>
> *'Ask him to move'.*

This negativity also included instances of non-cooperation on the part of the member of staff. Examples of this were: not lowering the wheelchair entrance ramp, not locating the bus near to the kerb or not trying to understand people with obvious communication difficulties. More extreme examples included directly abusing the disabled passenger or collaborating in the actioning of a hate crime or incident. Here the range of negativity is illustrated:

> *I thought, where is this guy coming from? He went straight past the stop. I had to wheel myself along the road to get on the bus. All right, mistakes can happen but this was no mistake. I asked him if he was having trouble parking. Do you know what he said? He said, 'no, I just didn't fancy having you on my bus'. I looked at him as if he was an alien. I used a foul word and he pulled away from the stop before I could secure the chair in the dock [the wheelchair bay].*
>
> *I should have known there was going to be trouble. You can tell when the bus is pulling-in. the face of the driver tells you a lot. This one looked like she had been chewing on a wasp. She kneeled the bus and shouted 'come on then, you're holding us up' I was polite. I said 'sorry'. She must have thought that people with sticks are also deaf because she said under her breath 'for fuck sake, fucking crippled shits' and started driving away. When I got off I wished her a lovely day …*
>
> *… I have trouble talking to people. They must take time to understand what I am saying … it's not my fault. I was asking the Guard if it stopped at XXX. He shouted so that everyone could hear. 'You must speak clearly'. I put my head down and tried again. He said 'You must speak clearly' again. All my life I have wanted to speak clearly. He looked at the other passengers in the carriage,*

it was packed. He said, 'I can't understand a word, who do they think I am a mind reader'? Now you know why I hate travelling by train.

Participants declared that the attitudes of staff have a direct impact on whether the incident itself is reported, or not. If a staff member were to encourage or solicit reports from the public, participants speculated that incident reporting would become more attractive. The research found that 28% of participants tried to report incidents. These were reported either to staff or to the police but, disappointingly, only 30% of these were followed up. Subsequently, only 8% of these reports were concluded to the participant's satisfaction. The majority of participants related that they were feeling too weak to report the situation either at the time or immediately afterwards. They considered that reporting was either a fruitless process or they did not know how to report such matters. Overwhelmingly, their thoughts were primarily focused on relief that the incident was finally over, and many felt that they wanted to return to the sanctuary of their homes and forget the matter. Here is one example:

No. I was just pleased to get home it really takes it out of you, you feel so tired. But I was so sad, I was in tears.

However, some participants did report the matter, either because they felt that justice needed to be served or in an attempt to forestall future attacks. These participants were generally angry at being targeted in such a public way. An, albeit rare, example of a satisfactory resolution is here:

I wrote to the (XXX) Metro and they were good. They found the CCTV evidence. They asked how they could help me, excellent, brilliant …

As stated above, only 8% of reports were satisfactorily resolved. Here are some examples of unresolved reporting:

If you can tell me the point of reporting something I will do it. I can't see the point. I have had twenty-plus attacks on me. I have reported about ten of them. I have never, never, never had a single positive feedback. I have never had anyone say sorry about that, we will look in to it. of the ten, or so, I reported they rang back once.

[Researcher] This was the company?

Yes, XXX Buses. If you complain about the service you don't get a reply so why should they care about his?

The man on the phone asked if I was joking. I said do you really think I would waste my time ringing you up to joke? He was no help—I had wasted my morning—he was the joke.

But when I was talking to people at the university about this I wasn't believed. I went to counselling and wasn't believed I am now so against counselling.

I complained to the police about this saying that someone was taking my picture without my permission. And that she was staring at me disturbingly.

...

[Researcher] And did the police come back to you?

...

No – not at first.

...

... But the officer then accused me of photographing this horrible child. And the police said that they couldn't help me at the time because it was a Saturday night and that they were busy. But after he asked to inspect my phone and I let him do it he said that I was intolerant of children. I said 'no I'm intolerant of badly behaved children and that's different'. I was the victim of a hate crime after all.

One participant reported the matter to a local newspaper after suffering many years of abuse on public transport. However, this produced subsequent victimisation:

Yeah. Well we've gone to papers; we've done loads of stuff around here. But we get the backlash, we get beat up because we reported it.

Most episodes of hate crimes or incidents however went unreported. When participants were asked why did not report these incidents, the following examples were offered:

No. Drivers are too busy just driving the bus.

No. To whom? When you get to London there's a scramble you don't want to talk to anyone about something daft.

[Researcher: Did you report the matter?]

...

What, that I had shit myself, what do you think?

Who do you report it too? The police don't want to know. If you get burgled they don't want to know.

There would have been no point. If the staff are so badly trained – as we [an independent living group] suspect – then what would they do with your report?

> *What would they do with your sensitive information? Do they have time to report these things and who to? How would they actually deal with your reports?*

Moreover, three participants were too scared to report these matters. Here is one example:

> *These were big men; they were going to beat up other men. They were going to do real damage and I couldn't sit in a court room with them, they were big men. I was intimidated. They had so much power over me and I was uncomfortable. The man who touched me I didn't want to report him to the police because the police are not good at that sort of thing, with mental health.*

Only a fraction of reports then had successful outcomes. Most of the reports were met with either no response or a promise to follow up the incident which was never met.

It was unclear how many incidents referred to by participants additionally constituted a sexual offence. Questions regarding sexual offences were not directly asked, and only one participant disclosed that a serious sexual offence occurred during her ordeal of a disability hate attack. However, three participants, all female, were subjected to sexualised slurs during disability hate attacks. These demeaning acts mainly concerned with a perceived inability to have sex or questioning how victims were able to have a baby. The propensity for females to be at a higher risk of victimisation is asserted by Bones (2013; see also EHRC 2011), a factor which can lead to a reticence to use public transport (Gardner et al. 2017).

3.7 Summary of Chapter 3

This chapter has delved into the horrifying experiences which can often be suffered by disabled people when using public transport in the UK. The richness of these data captured in the original research justified the research methods involved and the inclusion of people with disabilities themselves in the study. Before my research was undertaken, so little was known regarding the impacts of hostility in public environments. In this chapter, these experiences have been brought to light. The everyday nature of this hostility has been presented. But capturing the abusive experience is not enough, and the chapter also exposed the immediate impact on victims and responses of victims to counter these incidents. Any practices of resilience and retaliation were however relatively rare. The phenomenon of fellow, and formerly unoffending, passengers allying themselves with the principal offender was also revealed through my study, although not all potential recruits allied themselves in abusing others. Many decided just to ignore the situation which exacerbated the effect of making the victim feel isolated. Frightening enough that one abuser can be responsible for making someone's journey so miserable but then to have other passengers joining in that abuse has been evidenced by most participants as being a truly horrifying experience.

At times where the victim felt quite alone and exhausted, their one hope might be help from members of staff. My research found that almost all staff were unwilling to help or simply did not know how to help. The reporting of incidents was chiefly fruitless. The failure of most staff members to assist could reflect that public transport providers don't care about disabled passengers. The following chapter will examine the short- and long-term impacts of abuse and hostility on the victims and their associates including enforced lifestyle change.

Bibliography

Bones, P. (2013). Perceptions of Vulnerability: A Target Characteristics Approach to Disability, Gender, and Victimisation. *Deviant Behavior, 34*(9), 727–750.

Equality and Human Rights Commission (EHRC). (2011). *Hidden in Plain Sight: Inquiry into Disability-Related Harassment.* Manchester: Equality and Human Rights Commission.

Garcia, V. (2018, March 9). An Interview Between the Researcher and Victoria Garcia, Accessibility and Communities Manager for Brighton and Hove Buses and Metrobus.

Gardner, N., Cui, J., & Coiacetto, E. (2017). Harassment on Public Transport and Its Impacts on Women's Travel Behaviour. *Australian Planner, 54*(1), 8–15.

CHAPTER 4

The Victim: Lifestyle Impact and Change

Abstract This chapter reveals the shorter- and the longer-term impacts which befall the victims of disability hate crimes. In this chapter the immediate impact of being publicly abused is illustrated. The chapter then focuses on the longer-term impacts which, as with the author's experience, can continue to pervade the lives of the victims for decades. This profound fear and psychological disturbance often results in limited social skills and lifestyle constraints. These restrictions include abandoning public transport to avoid future abuse. Such abandonment has led to social exclusion, loneliness and restricted medical and employment opportunities. The ramifications of this abuse then are much wider and more prolonged than the immediate impacts.

Keywords Psychological impact • Coping strategies • Abandoning public transport • Social exclusion • Short-term • Long-term • Resilience

4.1 Chapter Introduction

This chapter introduces material which came to light subsequent to my original research. My main study captured the experiences of disability hate crime victimisation suffered by disabled people using public

D. Wilkin, *Disability Hate Crime*, Palgrave Hate Studies,
https://doi.org/10.1007/978-3-030-28726-9_4

transport services within the UK. Areas of focus which were revealed included the techniques used by abusers, the immediate impacts of the hostility and any tactical resilience employed by the victims. Also exposed was evidence of collaboration between the principal abuser and prospective allies in fashioning this abuse. Following the completion of my formal research, evidence from victims continued to reach me through a series of personal interactions. These come via email contact, through contact initiated through the Disability Hate Crime Network in the UK and during personal representations at meetings and lectures which I had conducted. I was under the misapprehension that these inputs would at least slow down following the conclusion of the main body of my research; however, they keep coming. Because of my relatively relaxed schedule which followed the original research, I found that more time could be allocated to understanding the longitudinal impacts of this abuse and hostility.

This chapter is therefore an opportunity to reveal the impacts and lifestyle changes encountered by victims and therefore represent the enduring impact of the abuse which they had suffered. In the first section, focusing on shorter-term impacts, the repercussions of the abuse in the days and weeks immediately following the incidents will be explored. The subsequent section, concerning the longer-term impacts, will look at the period following this, capturing the months following hostility and forward into the years ahead. The longer-term impacts will include accounts which include both explanations of resilience and coping and also evidence from those victims who are unable to cope with these longer-term impacts of hostility. It should be noted however that whilst this evidence relates to the recollection of historical incidents, many of the victims contributing to this chapter continue to face ongoing abuse. All direct quotations are *italicised*, and the contributing victims and witnesses identities have been anonymised.

4.2 Shorter-Term Impacts of Hostility

Perhaps when incidents of hate or hostility are discussed, there might perhaps be a tendency not to consider any effects on the witnesses to these events. In my original research witnesses were however included. Within UK law, witnesses have an equivalent right, alongside victims, to report hate incidents and crimes. Police guidance states that these reports should be accepted by the police as criminal incidents or acts (College of Policing [CoP]

2014). Many accounts were given to me by people accompanying the disabled person in the roles of personal assistants, carers, friends and chaperones. However, unconnected bystanders also came forward to give their evidence. Disbelief regarding the witnessed events was a common reaction from witnesses; they just could not believe that such incidents could occur, as one male onlooker corroborates:

> *It was unbelievable, my legs were like jelly, it was nothing to do with me, I wasn't the victim yet I really felt for her. I still think about it now.*

A female witness was afraid to intervene:

> *It's not nice to watch but if I say something then they'll turn on me. I think about it afterwards, I've seen it a few times, if I should have gone to help. But if they picked on me I'll be just another statistic wont I? I feel guilty but at the end of the day I'm safe. I wrestle with my conscience if you like.*

Members of public transport staff witness incidents as part of their daily routine. This male bus driver added his experiences:

> *OK I'm in charge. I'm the one. I drive the bus, collect the fares, I am an ambassador for the company and all of that. I'm told to keep myself safe so I don't [intervene in incidents]. What would happen if I did? A three-way [conflict]? I have the piss taken out of me almost every day that I work. Who do I run to--nobody. Life is tough at times. I feel sorry for 'em but, well, there ya' go. Nobody gives me counselling.*
>
> *What do you tell anyone? You can see some disturbing things that go on. But come on, I have too many things to do anyway. I get bollocked if I run late, I get bollocked if there is any complaint about me and I get bollocked if I'm deviating from anything that I should do. I sit there feeling like an idiot. What can I do and what should I have done? I think, if I report this, who do I tell and who would be interested anyway. I feel guilty, fine, I do. But I can't let it play on my mind for ever.*

During other incidents, family members had to suffer the indignity of watching their loved ones being the subject of abuse. Whether, or not, the witness was connected with the victim of the hostility, there was a general disposition to not retaliating on behalf of the disabled victim. It is also noteworthy that although not the primary target of abuse, those escorting the disabled person were themselves victims of emotional upset:

… constantly seeing this prejudice. I wonder how my wife can take so much. I can't. I know that she feels weak after an attack, I am weak too. I stand by and watch. My wife understands. I don't want to interfere. I feel I have failed as a man and to protect my wife.

My son gets 'oohs' and 'arghs' from the other bus passengers. I suppose they think they are being sympathetic. He's done so well and can, at least, walk, but he walks slowly and awkwardly. When we get home he can't understand why people have given him this supposed sympathy and this takes a long time to explain and he still doesn't get it.

[Researcher] What about the hate incidents?

Children and youngsters, mainly, make snide comments about his walking. He [the son] asks me what they mean. The trouble is, I don't know whether to tell him, or not. Do I prepare him for the rigors of a lifetime of these comments or just pretend that they are jokes? He's only seven after all. When his dad takes him out his dad gets angry and shouts how it is not XXX's [the son's] fault. But when they get home XXX wants to know why his daddy gets so angry—he wants to understand and I understand that. What do I do though?

It is therefore important to glean from these statements that witnesses to incidents are often as deeply affected as the disabled victims themselves. Moreover, these associates have themselves been targeted seemingly because of their association with a disabled person.

Aside from the witnesses, the majority of declarations concerning the shorter-term impacts were from directly victimised disabled people. Some of the immediate reactions to being abused are contained within Chap. 3. However, in the aftermath of an incident, when thoughts have been collected, sometimes the full realisation of what actually happened can come to mind:

I tried to get away from there as ASAP. It would be easy to try and work out [in the aftermath] if I could have handled it better, of course it would. But this would take time and would bring back the event. What I tend to do [instead] is sit in my [wheel]chair and try to relax. Sometimes I sit there for ten minutes, just thinking.

I'm tired today. I'm extra tired when it [an incident] happens to me. I know that my husband can't cope. I know that it stretches his heart and that he feels so useless. What would he do though? He's supposed to be my protector and I see a tear coming from his eye as he looks down and away. What can he do when it happens? What can he do afterwards? What's the point in retaliating? Afterwards I feel like having a hot bath, I feel violated and I can only guess what XXX [her husband] feels.

I'm nervous of talking 'cos I sound different. So if I'm at a bus I go upstairs if there is an upstairs and sit there alone. I don't talk to anyone then no one knows me and what I sound like. Later, I don't want to talk about anything like what happens.

[Researcher] You're' speaking OK now, how bad is your speech?

I get tongue-tied they say. I get mixed up.

I'll tell you what I do. I sit in my chair when I get home and cry. Sometimes I cry for days on—and—off. It's so unfair. Why should I be their target? … Crying doesn't solve anything of course. It doesn't heal me of their contempt of me. I don't feel better afterwards, but it's me …

… I'm so angry! So bloody angry! Every time I'm going to write and complain but who do you complain to? I wonder if I should tell the police, especially when I've been physically pushed or something. Is that assault? But in the end I tell no-one. If I did I would spend half of my life complaining. I cannot do that. So I stay angry for about three days. Them I'm better, then it happens again. It's like a circle.

of course these people put my pictures on Facebook [pictures of the victim]. Even if I wanted to get away from it, I couldn't. I watched these pictures being circulated and commented-on. Big smiley faces [emoticons] and thumbs-up. Big likes [Facebook 'likes']! Once it's on there it's on there. If I can't sleep I wonder how many people are out there looking at those pictures of me and thinking that I'm a cripple and a paedophile? Have they gone across the world? Will someone look at me in the street and whisper about me "that's him over there, the paedo". This shit is there for ever and a day, all about me.

You don't really get a chance to bounce back because it happens again. What is the point in trying to get over it? Tactically it might be better just to accept it and keep moving-on. I served in the British Army in Northern Ireland. Insults and shit were common as was spitting, glass in sandwiches and pots of piss being thrown at you. I can't let these people get to me. But I'm paraplegic and I need space and the freedom to move.

The examples given in this section represent the tip of an evidential iceberg of incidents related to me. Choosing the best examples to provide the most accurate representation of what happens to victims in the aftermath is problematic. Generally speaking, the shorter-term impacts seem only to last for days or weeks following the incident. However, contributors related that these impacts may also emerge into longer-term effects which are then experienced over prolonged periods of a victim's life, a characteristic which I can wholeheartedly endorse. These longer-term impacts will be discussed in the following section.

4.3 Longer-Term Impacts of Hostility

Some victims and witnesses face only the shorter-term impacts whilst some only the longer-term consequences. However, then there are the victims who face both types of impact. This section focuses on those longer-term impacts of hostility and abuse. Aside from lasting over a prolonged period of a victim's life, these seemingly cause deeper upset at the time and have more impactful repercussions throughout life. Many participants had developed techniques of resilience, and here are some examples which have been adopted by victims:

I think that you have to develop a strategy, a kind of Teflon [low-adhesion, non-stick, cookware] approach. You need to be thick-skinned like a suit of armour. If you really pondered about these attempts to derail your life, your life would be worth less than it is. I can't let them do that! Sometimes it gets to me but I don't linger on it. I can't do that.

Ha, I put a Pound in a pot every time it happens to me. That way I make a profit out of their [the abusers] ignorance.

I don't tend to think about what happens immediately after. But having said that, I it might just hit me a few weeks or months later. I'd be doing something quite ordinary like sleeping or something. Then suddenly, you know what I mean, you just get shit. The whole shit comes in to your mind in a flood and without warning, all the details and everything. I don't know what brings it on. My way of getting over it is to start shouting. Not at anyone in particular—but just replaying the situation with me as the hero this time. I give them hell! I tell them what I think of them and how fucking useless they are as human beings. My finger wags as well ... I suppose it's sad really because I don't say any of this to their faces. It makes me feel better though. But it's nowhere near to getting justice I suppose.

I practice yoga ... Yoga is great for making you in charge of your mind and your body. I rid myself of these angry sad people. I get to actually feel sorry for them. That's the way I cope with things.

Christianity stops me from being harmed by evil acts. I forgive, forgiveness is a great gift and I like to give it. I give it with the hope that these people [the abusers] will get better and start to give back to society what they got from it.

Most contributors had not, or could not, adopted techniques of resilience however and continue to be upset by incidents; examples of these follow:

What do you gain from being upset about these things? I keep asking myself that and telling myself not to be [upset] but I can't manage it. I can't do it. I still do get upset, and really badly as well. I think it's so unfair and wrong. Why do people, some people, think that they have a right to make things so bad for others? I don't do it to them or anything. What they do not realise is that they don't just ruin my day—they ruin my life. Every now and then thoughts come back to me of what they did and what they said. It may seem to be a small thing to them—a throw-away remark—and they probably forget what they said, like, two minutes afterwards. But to me it's deeply personal and I object to that. Horrible words and actions. I wet myself as well as not being able to move much. I have a PA [personal assistant]. But all of the comments about how people feel sick when they are near to me, pretending to throw-up [vomit] and holding their noses quite deliberately so I can see them do it. It's disgusting to me, it really is.

I avoid using the trams now. I talk funny and I get hurt for it. I don't like being hurt. It hurts me. I don't go no more.

It would be nice to have a choice but unfortunately I need to work. My powerchair is quite bulky but I have no alternative at all but to use it. And I know that there's going to be a pram in the wheelchair space [on the bus]. And I know that half of them are either going to refuse to move or make such an effort of moving in the hope that I will give up asking. I'm sure they hope that I'll feel bad about asking them—but I don't! I also know that many of them are going to be abusive, you can see them seethe. I hate conflict, I really do. But my alternative is not to go to work and not pay my bills, as if that is going to happen. No Miss, you'll just have to get out of the way, and now! As I say I don't like conflict but you have to be tough to survive and survive I will! But it's true to say that it does wear me down; most days are the same because I travel when the mummies are taking their cherubs to nursery of whatever. But I get fed up with having to run this gauntlet. Why should I be the victim of other people's lifestyle choices? Sometimes their prams are as big as my powerchair. I need my chair like they need their status symbols. The journey is so depressing I would love to kick it into touch. Such fucking shit!

The train and the Tube[1] *are the worst places for me. Because I get anxious and because my anxiety is really visible to others—that just makes me worse. I have been victimised in the past. That always plays on my mind that it could happen again and on any day. I should be ready for it when it comes but I never am. I don't handle it. If it happens I go to pieces. I have to get off of the train, I have to. I have to collect myself and try again. Sometimes I need to alight two or three times to get home. I know that I can't cope with it but my journey is a necessity. I'm not in control of my life.*

My sister lives in XXX. But I don't see her any more. It's not worth it as I can ring. I used to turn up in tears and she would ask me what was going-on.

[1] The Tube was a colloquial term and is now accepted branding for the London Underground transit mode operated by Transport for London.

Unless you have experiences it what is the point of telling anyone? I don't want her to see me all upset so I don't go anymore.

I rarely go out at all now. Not on the bus or Tube at all. It is just such hard work. I'm worn out just trying to use public transport at all. But not only that but I've been followed, only once, but it puts you off for ever; I've been followed back home by two guys who had already abused me on the bus. They live nearby, I know who they are, and the fact that they live so close makes me weep. Actually I cry all the time, or at least it feels like it. I get my groceries delivered. They said that they were going to smash my windows if I reported anything, so I haven't. It's terrifying! What am I supposed to do?

Is it worth it? This is supposedly a digital world. I have almost everything here. Apart from any friends, any contact anyone to speak to anyone to joke with and gossip with. You need that human touch and contact.

4.4 Summarising Chapter 4

This chapter has developed an understanding of the victim and witness experience of hostility. It has moved from the recounting of the practicality of incidents of hostility and abuse against disabled people on public transport. Instead, it has focused briefly on the aftermath, the ramifications of that mistreatment and the continuing upset. Distinctive themes have emerged from this chapter. This chapter has included the shorter-term impacts and coping strategies of victims who just pause for thought or flee the scene and hope for feelings of safety and security to be re-commenced. These strategies included the replaying of incidents once in the safety of one's own home so that *virtual revenge* can be meted out. In the longer-term impacts, the disappointment from victims was noteworthy in that they remain unable to cope despite being a victim of hate hostility on numerous occasions and, in some cases, in the distant past. Evident from the contributions is the power of the ongoing impacts and the depth of sustained harm which victims are unable to shake off. It is demonstrable that hate hostility produces profoundly alarming psychological disturbance across a range of victims and witnesses for protracted periods of time.

Bibliography

College of Policing (CoP). (2014). *Hate Crime Operational Guidance*. Coventry: College of Policing.

CHAPTER 5

The Safeguarding of Passengers on UK Public Transport

Abstract Hostility against disabled people on public transport in the UK is known as a problem by national government agencies. The data within this chapter will ascertain exactly what the public transport authorities and service providers are doing to safeguard disabled, and other passengers, from being abused. There are specific equality statutes in the UK to protect groups like disabled people. Data from 28 authorities and 53 service providers combined with staff interviews were used to reveal how earnestly, or not, this predicament is being dealt with. Enquires produced scant responses revealing that safeguarding policies and compliance with the law are rare. Poor collaboration at national government level continuing through to local and regulatory authorities prevails. Service providers are also not being equality-compliant and staff members are not being sufficiently trained to manage abusive situations. The result is disabled passengers not having the protection that they are entitled to.

Keywords Safeguarding • Regulatory authorities • Legal duty • Equality • Protection

5.1 Chapter Introduction

The main thrust of my research was to use a qualitative methodological approach to explore the experiences of disabled people suffering hostility whilst they used public transport in the UK. The findings from my study

D. Wilkin, *Disability Hate Crime*, Palgrave Hate Studies,
https://doi.org/10.1007/978-3-030-28726-9_5

uncovered the type of abuse suffered, the immediate responses of the victims and the long- and short-term impacts of this hostility. These facets were explored in Chaps. 3 and 4. The victim experience was however not the only focus of my research. Along with familiarity of the consequences of the problem, there was also a need to understand the measures that public transport authorities and service providers were taking to alleviate it. Therefore, to facilitate this, there was a fundamental need to understand the parameters concerning safeguarding the public which apply to the agencies overseeing public transport in the UK and the companies which provided the services. Lastly, and to provide a fully rounded appreciation, the study needed to know what public transport staff members knew of the problem and of how to manage it. Consequently, staff members were interviewed to provide an understanding of their level of knowledge regarding passenger safeguarding practises and to gauge how confident they were in applying these practices. In summary, the question that is being asked within this chapter is: just how competent are public transport authorities and providers at safeguarding disabled people when they use public transport?

5.2 Oversight

In the UK, public transport services are usually provided by private companies. They may be relatively small or part of national or international conglomerates. These companies can be contracted to provide these services by regulatory or local authorities. Local authorities in the UK, at town, county, district and regional levels, are usually also responsible for the provision and management of municipal services and the provision of bus stops and public transport interchange facilities. These authorities are therefore influential partners in the licencing, planning and the provision of transport services within their areas. Furthermore, they fund public transport services when these are commercially unviable, for example, on Sundays or to remote areas. They also provide specialist transit services for people with certain needs: schoolchildren, people with special educational needs and so on. Conversely, regulatory authorities focusing on public transport, often entitled Passenger Transport Executives (PTEs), specifically oversee and regulate public transport services. Additionally, but rarely, they can themselves manage infrastructure and can directly contract out public transport provision to private companies. Specific responsibilities vary depending on location. Both local and regulatory authorities often participate in bus partnerships in striving to achieve a multi-agency approach to service planning and other partnerships, for example, to discuss crime control and anti-social behaviour.

To ascertain if local and regulatory authorities were taking their responsibilities to safeguard disabled and other passengers seriously, my research raised 28 requests under the UK Freedom of Information (FOI) Act 2000 (FOI Act). This FOI Act obliges such public agencies to respond candidly to requests for information within 20 working days. An FOI request was also sent to the UK government's Department for Transport (DfT). To ascertain how public transport service providers safeguard their passengers, 53 further written requests for information were made directly to these companies. The FOI Act could not be used for these requests as private companies are involved, and they are therefore exempt from the FOI Act. Unless, that is, they were a wholly owned subsidiary of a local authority or regulatory body, a situation which is relatively rare.

The statutory equality responsibilities of authorities and service providers are clearly established within section 149 of the Equality Act 2010 in a provision called the Public Sector Equality Duty (PSED). The PSED is clear in that any agency or company conducting activities of a public nature, as defined within the Human Rights Act 1998, must adhere to the principles of the PSED. This provision makes it clear for all agencies contracting, supplying, influencing or overseeing public services that they have statutory obligations to eliminate: discrimination, harassment, victimisation and other prejudiced conduct prohibited by the Equality Act. Additionally, they have a duty to advance equality of opportunity between persons who share relevant *protected* characteristics and those who do not and furthermore to foster good relations between these groups. Protected characteristics include all categories of people covered by the Equality Act, one of which is disabled people. The overseeing agencies must also publish their equality objectives and publish an annual report regarding progress and development towards meeting these objectives. The PSED must be applied at all levels of these organisations from board level downward. It must also be applied to those agencies and companies which are subordinate to it. Appropriate training must be given to staff at both authority and subordinate levels to raise their understanding of these equality issues. The only release from commitments contained within the PSED is if the cost implications of equality are prohibitive. The PSED also applies to any public service procured or commissioned by any of the regulatory bodies or local authorities. It is therefore an all-consuming

Act and PSED covering public functions and cannot be delegated. The Equality and Human Rights Commission (EHRC) is responsible in the UK for oversight of the Equality Act and therefore the PSED and for addressing non-compliance. At the time of interviewing the Head of the Cross-government Hate Crime programme in 2017, the application of the PSED by public transport authorities and service operators had not been enforced by the EHRC and had not been tested in court (Giannasi 2017). At the time of writing this book (summer 2019), no evidence of any enforcement since that interview could be found.

5.3 Public Transport and Equality Policy

In the UK, the central government's Department for Transport insists that the responsibility for overseeing and influencing equality legislation amongst transport service providers rests firmly with the superintending authority when they are procuring, providing, licencing or contracting any service provider to operate any bus service within that authority's geographic area of responsibility. This duty also applies when authorities are establishing and managing bus or train interchange facilities. The rail franchise agreements serve the same purpose as far as railway services are concerned (FOI1 2018). Whilst the Office of Rail and Road (ORR) set the standards for the safeguarding of disabled people, these standards only act to ensure access ability to trains for passengers mainly with physical disabilities and blindness. They do not provide for the protection of equality rights for any protected group (Office of Rail and Road, 2018). Any policing of bus services is facilitated through neighbourhood policing teams resourced from within the county and regional police forces throughout the UK. The policing of the railway infrastructure rests with the British Transport Police (BTP). The DfT states that the enforcement of anti-hate crime policies is vested with these police forces (FOI1 2018). In 2018 the DfT published their *Inclusive Transport Strategy* (DfT 2018). This document was heavily aligned towards enabling physical accessibility for disabled people, in other words making public transport easier to use. However, it does also echo the UK government's commitment to reduce hate crime across all of its monitored strands and promises to continue to work with Deaf and Disabled People's Organisations (DDPOs) and the BTP to tackle hate crime. Moreover, it undertakes to provide an awareness campaign to commence in 2019–20 to increase public awareness of the illegality of committing hate crime acts (2018:47).

5.4 Questions to Local and Regulatory Authorities

To establish safeguarding procedures in place, the FOI requests to the authorities and regulatory bodies were couched as the following questions:

1. The Home Office strategy: Action Against Hate, 2016, indicates that public transport is a key area of concern for hate crimes being conducted towards people with disabilities. What action is your organisation taking to reduce hostility and abuse against people with disabilities on your public transport services in your area?
2. Please send me your policies and strategies for dealing with the potential for hostility and abuse against people with disabilities on public transport services in your area.
3. What training interventions do you stipulate or suggest to enable public transport staff be aware of, and manage, the potential of hostility and abuse against people with disabilities on public transport services in your area?
4. How does your organisation raise awareness of the possibility of hostility and abuse against people with disabilities on public transport services in your area?
5. Please send to me your published equality objectives in relation to public transport provision in your area and clarify how you make these objectives accessible to the public.
6. Please send me any progress that you have made towards meeting equality objectives concerning public transport in your area.
7. Please clarify how you incorporate the Public Sector Equality Duty in your provision of public transport including when contracts are agreed with contracting service operators.

5.5 Transparency of Freedom of Information Protocols

The responses to the FOI requests were noteworthy. Five of the responding authorities gave robust and detailed responses to most questions. Most authorities however stated that they did not possess the requested information. If these declarations were correct, this is indicative that these authorities: had no policies for dealing with equality issues at their bus interchanges; had not made any progress towards meeting equality objectives and do not publish an annual report regarding these objectives. All of which are requirements within the Equality Act 2010 and its associated PSED. Moreover, Transport for the North East (managed by NEXUS) failed to maintain a functioning email address through which to process such FOI requests (at the time of requesting, late 2018). Furthermore, Transport for the North—a recently empowered agency, formed in 2018 to integrate transport modes in the north of England—did not have established protocols to enable FOI enquiries. Generally, however, local authorities and PTEs responded with scant detail to the specific questions raised. Local authorities often indicated that public transport services in their areas were privately operated and therefore not the responsibility of that authority—a position which is obviously incorrect as local authorities often operate and manage bus interchanges and provide bus services at unpopular times and for specialist transportation and so on (Garcia 2018). Therefore, their involvement must be intrinsic. Conversely, the responses from the PTEs were more detailed and helpful, and the PTEs, whose role it is to oversee and regulate public transport operations, should arguably supply all-embracing answers to such requests. Written requests to public service providers, outside of the stipulations of the Freedom of Information Act 2000, were commonly met with no response at all. The only exceptions to this were Stagecoach South West, Plymouth Citybus, Brighton and Hove Buses, Lothian Buses and Edinburgh Trams. However, no responses were given by any source whatsoever was made indicating the annual reporting of PSED obligations.

5.6 Responses from Authorities

All of the authorities responding to FOI requests had established and publicly accessible equality policies. In some locations, these consisted of a broad aspiration to safeguard the public. One example of this was the South Yorkshire PTE. This authority took its responsibility to protect all members of the public seriously within the bus interchanges which it managed. It also worked with rail providers to offer similar safeguarding on railway premises. Plymouth City Council, NEXUS, Brighton and Hove City Council and Gateshead Council were good examples of where authorities worked closely with local operators to specifically reduce hate crime. NEXUS, in North East England, had produced a Hate Crime

Charter in October 2018 to itemise how it would protect susceptible passengers. Another example of a good-quality safeguarding partnership is that of Brighton and Hove City Council working closely with Brighton and Hove Buses to achieve passenger safeguarding (Garcia 2018). The City Council insists that its bus providers adopt equality training regimes and display publicity in its vehicles and interchanges to promote the anti-hate message. Other good examples came to light. Transport for Greater Manchester PTE utilised security patrols and poster campaigns to raise awareness and help manage hate incidents and crimes. Transport for London has, on its London Underground mode, training modules to raise awareness of hate incidents. In Edinburgh, the City Council and Police Scotland work in partnership to specifically drive down hate on its public transport. As a result of these efforts, service providers learned from enforcement and partner agencies about how to reduce hate crime and raise awareness of equality issues among its staff. Moreover, some providers had developed training interventions, not only to raise awareness of equalities and the hate problem but also to raise awareness of how to manage it.

Alternatively, and disappointingly, most of the remaining authorities did little towards achieving equality and nothing towards managing potential hate crimes or incidents. Most local authorities claimed that public transport was outside of their control. Focusing on bus services, most authorities stated that commercial providers operate these services, and therefore, the authorities were distanced from any operational detail. These distancing strategies are clearly problematic. Whether or not these authorities have equality policies in place, the denial of responsibility and the non-establishment of contractual equality obligations mean that these authorities do little or nothing towards safeguarding those facing hostility on public transport or therefore meeting their PSED obligations. Moreover, and further inferring denial of responsibility for service provision, some of the authorities receiving FOI requests forwarded the request to a local public transport operator for comment. In most cases, these forwarded requests were not responded to. This attitude towards hostility involving disabled victims may help to explain why, for example, 52% of people who, having faced hate attacks in the Leicester area were disappointed with responses from the police and other agencies (Chakraborti et al. 2014). This evidence additionally aligns with the proportionally small 8% of resolved complaints cited in my research.

5.7 Service Provider Responses

I had also contacted 53 bus and train service providers which produced only 6 direct responses and 2 more through redirected FOI requests. Because of the paucity of responses, all of these can be summarised within this section. Cross Country Trains (2018) and Virgin Trains East Coast (2018)[1] responded to my request speedily. They indicated that they have instituted policy, publicity and training to deal with hostility against disabled people on its services across the UK. However, on examining the supplied information, it focuses merely on the accessibility of disabled people to its services. The documents extol its workforce as having been trained in providing access to its trains and stations whenever possible and that staff members will be responsive to requests from disabled passengers. However, despite the specific nature of the FOI request, nothing was revealed by the companies referring to policies which related directly to hate crime, equalities, hostility or the reporting of such matters. Another speedy respondent was Nottingham Express Transit which operates trams within the city of Nottingham and to surrounding transit hubs. They were eager to confirm that they have not experienced reports of disability hate crime on their system. They also stated that if anyone is abused, they can operate a *Help Point* button and summon the assistance of the driver. However, it did not provide evidence towards any training concerning disability equality or hate crime. Neither did they provide advertising to make passengers aware of how to respond to abusive situations (Nottingham Express Transit 2018).

Plymouth Citybus alternatively works very closely with an anti-hate crime organisation called Stop Hate UK and has also taken part in the annual National Hate Crime Awareness Week anti-hate promotion which takes place in the UK during October. At these events Plymouth Citybus displayed posters and anti-hate crime publicity. Campaigns were pitched both internally to the company staff members and externally to the public. Also in Plymouth, Stagecoach South West was speedy to confirm its actions to reduce hate crime on its services. It gave a more comprehensive response which is worth reproducing in its entirety because of its detail:

> *We do have training related to hate crime; this is covered in two modules 'Disability and Equality Awareness' and 'Dealing with Difficult Situations'.*

[1] This company has now been superseded by London North Eastern Railways, protocols have however remained unchanged.

> *Both of these courses count toward a drivers' CPC entitlement and these courses are also part of every new driver's induction. The disability and equality training is quite focused on the Equality Act, and how this applied to a bus driver's role. Much of this is focused on customers with disabilities, for example the importance of ensuring the wheelchair space is vacated for a wheelchair user, offering assistance, hidden disabilities etc. There is also a discussion on diversity in the bus industry and society in general, be that related to race, sexual orientation and gender, religion etc. and there is also opportunity for discussion where drivers are encouraged to share their own experiences; hate crime is discussed at this point and drivers are encouraged to report issues where people have been targeted because of a protected characteristic. In the module 'Dealing with Difficult Situations' drivers are shown how to diffuse situations and act in a manner that protects them and the public (such as only challenging people where there is an escape route etc.), and in this module drivers are encouraged to report any situation where a customer (or the driver) has been the target of any unwanted comments. These reports would be sent directly to me and I would obtain evidence such as statements, CCTV etc. and also involve the police if necessary.* (FOI2 2018)

In addition, a full response was obtained from Brighton and Hove Buses, part of the national conglomerate the Go-Ahead Group; they remain the only bus operator in the UK to have an Accessibility and Communities Manager (Garcia 2018). This manager informed me that a strong and mutually successful partnership exists between Brighton and Hove City Council, the local police and themselves. Part of the bus company strategy ensures that one police officer is financially subsidised to take a special interest in crime aboard its buses and liaise with the company. Furthermore, Brighton and Hove Buses drivers receive regular training to maintain a high awareness of equality issues with a particular focus on disability. As part of their protocols, any driver who is subject of a complaint by a disabled person is given guidance as to their future conduct rather than being summarily disciplined (Garcia 2018). Additionally, all of Brighton and Hove Buses vehicles are fitted with two dedicated bays: one for disabled people with a separate one for baby buggies. Garcia (2018) cited that the senior executives of the company have close personal experience of disability and hate issues and that this had influenced their enlightened approach. Similarly, NEXUS, the Tyne and Wear regulatory passenger transit authority in North East England which also operates the Tyne and Wear Metro, worked with Gateshead Council and other local partners to produce videos giving public advice regarding disability hate crime and *mate crime* (Gateshead 2018). These are incidents where an abuser seemingly befriends the disabled person with a view to exploiting this relationship. Public transport can be a location where victims can be *befriended* for later manipulation. Furthermore, both the NEXUS front-line and control room staff members are trained to recognise these events and quickly report such incidents to the police. This work is supported by a local Hate Crime Charter for Public Transport (NEXUS 2018). This charter shows good leadership in its commitments towards supporting victims, raising staff awareness of hate issues, installing technology assets to monitor crime and engaging with local interest groups (Lewis 2019; NEXUS 2018). Also Lincolnshire County Council does train its drivers concerning equality issues where special or directly funded services operate—but, perhaps oddly—services with alternative funding do not receive the same attention.

To gain a distinctive perspective of how well public transport staff are prepared to understand and assist with hostility against disabled people, I conducted structured interviews with a sample of staff from rail and bus service operators in East Anglia, an eastern area of the UK including both rural and urban settings. I recognise that the limited scale of this survey does not make it scientifically representative but it should be noted that responses were difficult to acquire. However, any contributions from those who will be expected to manage such incidents of hostility are of value. In the responses to the interview questions, it was first evident that staff members did not know how to recognise people with some disabilities because these were indiscernible. They also stated that they did not have sufficient time within their duties to react with the appropriate help and that they were ill-prepared to do so. One bus driver notably thought that it was the work of the police to assist in such matters whilst another considered that all that was needed was a little compassion. One respondent stated that it was not his job to *nanny* people. However, all respondents indicated that sufficient training was not provided for dealing with situations of hostility against disabled people or their rights to equality. Most training that they did receive aligned with the Disability Awareness Training (DAT) model which included: manoeuvring a bus and deploying a ramp to help disabled people board and alight. On railway infrastructure, similar approaches included arranging for assistance and deploying train boarding ramps. In other words this training deals with accessibility issues. All respondents knew who to contact to report incidents. However, most respondents had little confidence in receiving any prompt assistance if they had to report such issues. Most of the contributors stated that they required better training to understand the needs of disabled people and the effects of hostility. One respondent understood what hate crime was; the remainder however did not. In other words training to the standard of Disability Equality Training (DET), which would have created learning around the rights and equality issues of disabled people, was desired by staff members. One other discovery from conducting the staff survey was that all participants were determined that their responses would be treated with complete anonymity. The entire cohort had a fear of subsequent retribution from employers should they be identified. One participant stated that his contract of employment contained a clause where he should not speak with 'outsiders' concerning his work.

5.8 Staff Training and Crime Reduction Strategies

All public service buses in the UK must provide space for both wheelchair use and priority seating. The Bus Services Act 2017 came into operation in the UK in March 2018. In its developmental phase the Act was discussed with various consultees with a view towards giving bus drivers authority to enforce wheelchair bay occupancy for disabled people using wheelchairs and remove those unwilling to allow this. However, the final Bill retained that obligation but without giving drivers the power to enforce it. However, later DfT guidance (DfT 2018) aspires to address this issue. The DfT claim that bus operators 'take disability awareness training amongst their drivers seriously' (FOI1 2018), which anyway is an obligation of the Bus Services Act 2017. Though as illustrated above, this training falls short of delivering the type of human rights awareness that only Disability Equality Training can provide. The 2017 Act obligates bus companies to deliver Disability Awareness Training to their drivers and supervisory staff during basic training and again during their annual Certificate of Professional Competence (CPC) re-licencing activity. Furthermore, DfT (2018) guidance states that this activity should include equality awareness training—but it falls short of either defining or demanding this. Delineation is helpful here of the two main types of training regimes available: Disability Awareness Training raises awareness of disability and focuses generally on access to the transport mode and to providing assistance. Some, limited, DAT provision focuses additionally on communication difficulties and passenger information for disabled passengers. Alternatively, Disability Equality Training is an enhanced package which delivers all of the things that DAT provides but additionally summarises the equality rights of disabled people and the inequalities which they face in their daily lives. This training would also be an opportune platform for hate crime and hostility management to be presented to front-line staff (Garcia 2018). Some UK operators, for example, Stagecoach South West, have bespoke training packages and have introduced *Disability and Equality Awareness* and *Dealing with Difficult Situations* (FOI2 2018). Other operators, for example, Lincolnshire special services, utilise modular training packages which can be rolled out to staff as required (FOI3 2018). Examples of providers of these packages, available at the time of writing, include: Centre for Hate Studies (2018) at the University of Leicester and Stop Hate UK (Stop Hate UK 2017a). A typical syllabus for DET is provided by Stop Hate UK, which covers the legal framework of hate crime, the impact of hate crime on victims, the nature of hate crime perpetrators and differences between victim groups. In more practical terms the traditionally low reporting rates are emphasised as are the available means of reporting hate crime. Successful intervention techniques and the importance of leadership to achieve equality goals are also part of the package (Stop Hate UK 2017b).

As can be seen from the example above, the emphasis moves within DET training from purely access and an understanding of physical needs, to one where equalities and human rights are additionally considered. The obligations of the Bus Services Act 2017 and the requirements of the DfT (FOI1 2018) both mandate training to be delivered to front-line staff. The DfT seeks that the effectiveness of this training is vital to public transport provision in that the positive outcomes from that training can only enhance the reputations of the operating companies. Furthermore, it recognises that this reputation is important to these companies (FOI1 2018). Professional repute is commercially important to these providers as many of the groups providing public transport in the UK: Abellio, FirstGroup, Stagecoach and Virgin are examples of companies with international standings who bid to provide public transport services across the globe. In a bidding round, reputation may be pivotal to being considered as the favoured provider.

Nevertheless, one apparent difficulty which might make the provision of training difficult to commercially justify is that no effective monitoring of training regimes currently exists in the UK to allow public transport providers to adequately evaluate the outcomes of staff learning. Companies may be reticent to commit to funding training if they cannot be reassured by any tangible results. One of the more unsubstantiated methods by which the effect of training is monitored is through customer satisfaction surveys. Rail-based examples of these are TfL (Transport for London) (2017) and Greater Anglia (2017), which are regular market research sweeps. These surveys often enquire about passenger perceptions of security whilst on railway premises. However, it is difficult to attribute any perceptions of enhanced security directly to training interventions.

Focusing on the raising awareness of hate crime on public transport, the DfT asserts that it is the clear responsibility of localised bus partnerships to promote this facet (FOI1 2018). However, there are more inconsistencies here; in one example (of many) from my research, Barnsley City Council, which is an active partner in a local Bus Partnership with South Yorkshire PTE, claims that they do not hold any information regarding these matters—despite the DfT placing the responsibility for doing so squarely on their shoulders (FOI4 2018; FOI5 2018). The DfT also indicate that many operators and local police forces participate together in events, for example, the UK-wide National Hate Crime Awareness Weeks. Indeed good work is evident, and the BTP additionally participated in monthly awareness sessions at locations across the UK rail network. However, many local police forces do not participate in such events to the same extent (BTP 2017).

Assuming that training has taken place, staff members need to have confidence that any incidents which they report will be dealt with swiftly; otherwise, these key personnel might be dissuaded from reporting such matters again in the future. The DfT in their guidance to rail franchisees espouses that rail providers must have arrangements in place to report the crime to the British Transport Police (FOI1 2018). Railway service providers however do not have any special or prioritised arrangements for contacting the police but instead use the same arrangements as any private citizen in that they call the 999 emergency telephone services. Larger rail providers have a dedicated line from their Sector, Signalling and Operations Controllers to the BTP Force Management Centres—but again this is only a standard telephone call and does not flag as any type of *priority*. These arrangements carry the risk of transit operators facing the same delays in reporting problems as those which might be encountered by the general public and therefore no guarantee of a speedy response to an evolving incident. Furthermore, and again problematically, county, specialist and regional police forces do not have any right—unless life is endangered—to enter railway premises unless formally invited to do so by the BTP. This means that local police have to wait at the threshold of the railway station until being asked to enter. Alternatively, the BTP, who are placed at strategic locations around the rail network, cannot operate outside of railway premises unless invited to do so by the local police force or, also, unless life is at risk. Furthermore, and again problematically, the BTP recognises that response times are poor in rural locations and therefore invites local forces to attend these locations as necessary (BTP 2017). However, a divisive relationship seems to exist between some local police forces and the BTP and is partially based upon the disparate nature of police funding in the UK (Giannasi 2017). The BTP is directly funded by the UK Home Office whereas county and regional forces are funded by county councils and local taxes. This relationship clearly cannot result in effective management of crime if resentment exists and strictly observed, demarcated areas of responsibility remain untraversed.

To summarise the complex issues raised within this section, training regarding disabled people is delivered to all bus drivers and to most rail staff, and this features disability awareness learning but not, generally speaking, equality awareness. Disability Equality Training which covers both the facets of accessibility and equality is not, in the main, delivered to public transport staff. The relationships between the BTP and local police forces incur some tensions around operational boundaries, and any intransigence cannot be helpful in tackling crime, especially in rural areas where response times must be much longer as they are further from where police officers are stationed. Reporting methods to police services offer no guarantee of a speedy response to any incident on public transport services, and this can result in staff members not having the confidence to continue reporting such incidents. Finally, although the DfT expects that local bus partnerships promote awareness of all crime, including hate crime, and to embed this in operator specifications, evidence of this happening is generally not available. This disparity of intention and action is, it seems, reflective of the low prioritisation of disability hate crime in the UK government and within local and regulatory authorities generally (Giannasi 2017).

5.9 Non-compliance with Legislation

Many years have elapsed since the establishment of the Equality Act 2010 and its associated PSED in the UK. In that time there seems to have been little positive impact from this legislation in its aspiration to protect equalities in the public arena (Giannasi 2017). Paul Giannasi, Head of the UK Cross-government Hate Crime Programme confirmed that the Equality Act and its PSED can only become more effective if cooperation and shared purpose improve between the Department for Transport and other government departments. The Government Equalities Office (2013) quantitative report on the successes of the PSED confirms that leverage may be necessary to induce agencies to take their responsibilities seriously. But it acknowledges that this had been difficult to activate in the past. They additionally recognise that more guidance is required to compel agencies and companies to use the PSED to its fullest (HM Government Equalities Office 2013:4–5). Furthermore, Giannasi asserted that the DfT and, similarly, the Department of Health and Social Care tend to work in silos and not to collaborate particularly well with other agencies (Giannasi 2017). Moreover, Giannasi thought that the implementation of any equality legislation is stymied further by the EHRC being a bureaucratic organisation which tends not to act with any urgency in enforcing the Equality Act. Giannasi also confirmed that hate crime on public transport was not being highly prioritised within the UK government despite a range of reports which suggest that it is a key criminogenic environment for these crimes. Giannasi also confirmed that to raise the profile of hate crime on public transport, specific questions should be placed into the Crime Survey for England and Wales to bring the resulting data to the attention of the UK government. Moreover, Giannasi stated that this was unlikely to happen as there was (at the time of the interview, late 2017) a waiting list of questions to be placed into that survey and that these queries had a greater priority in government circles (Giannasi 2017). Giannasi supplemented this by verifying that the relatively low priority of public transport hate crime has resulted in an absence of court actions against authorities or their contracted service providers. This evidence, from the person at the very top of UK governmental policy regarding hate crime, substantiates the evidence of non-action garnered from public transport authorities and providers.

This inaction is further demonstrated at local and regional levels with regard to public transport provision. Of the 28 regulatory agencies and local authorities which were subject to FOI requests, only 1 directly answered seventh question regarding the PSED; the question was:

> Please clarify how you incorporate the Public Sector Equality Duty in your provision of public transport including when contracts are agreed with contracting service operators?

South Yorkshire PTE responded to this question by stating that bus operators under their supervision are obliged to provide evidence that they comply with the PSED in their service operations (FOI4 2018). This evidence might, for example, merely refer to the way that they provide travel information and how they maintain customer service standards. They added that they oversee three bus partnership arrangements co-managed with local authorities. These arrangements, the PTE claim, incorporate facets of accessibility, information and customer service. One particular example is a partnership with Barnsley City Council. However, the PTE response is inconsistent with that from Barnsley City Council. In a similar distancing technique to that used by other local authorities, it inexplicably denies having anything to do with the establishment or operation of bus services in its area (FOI5 2018). South Yorkshire PTE also advised me that they had entered into a disability partnership with local rail operators to deliver better access and information (FOI4 2018). Whilst this sole response to the PSED question was meritorious, it did not however address the ongoing problem of hostility against disabled people which was the specific theme of the FOI questions asked. The paucity of response to this question within the FOI requests is indicative of localised disinterest, and this potentially reflects the UK government's low priority towards addressing hostility against disabled people on buses and trains as illustrated by Giannasi (2017). Despite the wealth of evidence suggesting that disabled people are socially isolated, suffering poor access to education and economically challenged there seem to be no priority within government, regulator or provider circles to effect change.

5.10 Summarising Chapter 5

The purpose of this chapter has been to ascertain the strategies in place to safeguard disabled passengers whilst travelling on the UK's public transport services. FOI and other written requests were made to authorities and to companies which provide these services. They all share a duty under the Equality Act 2010 and its subsidiary regulation the PSED to keep all of their passengers safe and to be inclusive towards the diversified needs of these customers. They additionally have a duty to work positively in promoting equality between diverse groups and to produce equality goals, policies and performance publicity as a demonstration of their ambition to do this. Moreover, public service regulators and providers have a duty to enshrine equality in all of its procurement, contracts, training and procedures. Some of the responders to the FOI requests did not meet the spirit of the Freedom of Information Act 2000 by failing to provide direct responses. The questions which were posed were directly aligned to hate crime and hostility against disabled people on public transport. Despite this, many of the responding agencies answered with information about access to transport services and, on rare occasions, equality in general terms. Aside that is from NEXUS, Plymouth City Council, Transport for Greater Manchester, Edinburgh Trams, Gateshead Council, Edinburgh City Council, South Yorkshire PTE, Transport for London and Brighton and Hove City Council, most other FOI responders seemed to have little knowledge and a shortage of policy concerning hate crime on public transport. One respondent proudly cited that it complied with outdated legislation. A few of the remaining FOI respondents did allude to having produced some publicity to raise awareness of the hostility problem. However, this did not specifically concern disabled people nor did it concern public transport. It can be inferred from this data trawl that the hate crime on public transport is not fully understood or that if it is, policies were yet to be put into place. It is also indicative that only one of the respondents clearly replied regarding its compliance with the PSED.

Disappointingly, most of the public transport service providers questioned did not respond to my requests for information either. Staff working on public transport services provided by Brighton and Hove Buses (Garcia 2018), Tyne and Wear Metro (Gateshead 2018), Stagecoach South West, Plymouth Citybus (FOI2 2018), London Underground and within the Manchester (FOI6 2018), Blackpool (FOI7 2018), NEXUS (Lewis 2019; NEXUS 2018) and Edinburgh (FOI8 2018; FOI9 2018) areas however seemed to be prepared, to varying extents, to manage hostility against disabled people. Bus drivers in the Brighton and Hove and Blackpool areas, for example, have additionally had excellent preparation for dealing with these matters. Brighton and Hove Buses boasted the only Accessibility and Communities Manager in any UK bus company at the time of writing (Garcia 2018). Moreover, Brighton and Hove Buses acknowledge that the ever-changing social *milieu* requires constantly evolving training regimes to cope with passenger needs and expectations. Garcia is also aware of the problem of abusers recruiting formerly unoffending passengers referred to in Chap. 6 of this book as Collaborative Alienation (Garcia 2018). Evidence from the public transport staff interviews substantiates the evidence from the 28 authorities and the responses from service providers. These indicate an overwhelming scarcity of awareness regarding hostility and hate crime. Furthermore, staff members questioned did not feel that they had been prepared to manage such incidents, although staff on rail services—where the fewest attacks occur—were better placed to contact operational support staff and to request assistance if required. However, they also stated that they had little confidence in receiving a speedy police response from the police, if requested. Bus drivers in particular neither understood the need to help nor had the confidence to intervene concerning hate offences.

Also evident within this chapter is the disjointed approach in the governance of improving equalities for disabled passengers. Giannasi (2017) asserted that government departments are not commonly allied in their approaches to tackling these problems and no urgency is being applied to collect relevant data via national crime and victim surveys to establish the breadth of any problem. Moreover, the EHRC is not ensuring the compliance of authorities and providers with any urgency.

The following chapter will take the findings from Chaps. 3 and 4 alongside this chapter and discuss these against academic literature, legal duty and expectations; in doing so, that chapter will align some patterns of offending with known and emerging theorisation.

Bibliography

British Transport Police (BTP). (2017, August 3). *Interview Between the Author and Inspector Granville Sellers, Deputy Lead for Hate Crimes, of the BTP Safeguarding Hub*. Leeds: British Transport Police.

Centre for Hate Studies. (2018). *Training*. Leicester: The University of Leicester. Online at: https://le.ac.uk/hate-studies/training. Accessed 27 Dec 2018.

Chakraborti, N., Garland, J., & Hardy, S.-J. (2014). *The Leicester Hate Crime Project: Findings and Conclusions*. Leicester: University of Leicester.

Cross Country Trains. (2018). *Email Response from Customer Service Team XC180116BC5V Received on 22nd January 2018*. Sunderland: Cross Country Trains.

Department for Transport. (2018). *The Inclusive Transport Strategy: Achieving Equal Access for Disabled People*. London: Department for Transport.

FOI1. (2018). *Freedom of Information Response from the Department for Transport (DfT) Ref: F0015633 Received 30/1/18*. London: Department for Transport (DfT).

FOI2. (2018). *Freedom of Information Response from Plymouth City Council Ref: 896614 Received 20/2/18*. Plymouth: Plymouth City Council.

FOI3. (2018). *Freedom of Information Response from Lincolnshire County Council Ref: 46462118FOI, Received 30/07/2018.* Lincoln: Lincolnshire County Council.

FOI4. (2018). *Freedom of Information Response from South Yorkshire Passenger Transport Executive (PTE) Ref: SR8365 Received 20/2/18.* Sheffield: South Yorkshire Passenger Transport Executive (PTE).

FOI5. (2018). *Freedom of Information Response from Barnsley Metropolitan Borough Council Ref: FOIA 1746 Received 25/01/2018.* Barnsley: Barnsley Metropolitan Borough Council.

FOI6. (2018). *Freedom of Information Response from Transport for Greater Manchester Ref: 2018/0007 Received 13/2/18.* Manchester: Transport for Greater Manchester.

FOI7. (2018). *Freedom of Information Response from Blackpool Council Ref: 180052/F3 Received 13/02/2018.* Blackpool: Blackpool Council.

FOI8. (2018). *Freedom of Information Response from Edinburgh Trams Ref Unknown Received 19/2/18.* Edinburgh: Edinburgh Trams.

FOI9. (2018). *Freedom of Information Response from Lothian Buses Ref Unknown Received 20/2/18.* Edinburgh: Lothian Buses.

Garcia, V. (2018, March 9). An Interview Between the Author and Victoria Garcia, Accessibility and Communities Manager for Brighton and Hove Buses and Metrobus.

Gateshead Council. (2018). *Recognising and Reporting Hate Crime (Short Films).* Online at: https://www.gateshead.gov.uk/article/6434/Recognising-and-Reporting-Hate-Crime-short-films-.Accessed 6 Mar 2019.

Giannasi, P. (2017, September 20). *Interview at the UK Home Office Between the Author and Paul Giannasi Head of the Cross-Government Hate Crime Programme.*

Greater Anglia. (2017). *Customer Satisfaction Survey.*

HM Government Equalities Office. (2013). *The Independent Steering Group's Report of the Public Sector Equality Duty (PSED): Review and Government Response.* Online at: https://www.gov.uk/government/publications/the-independent-steering-groups-report-of-the-public-sector-equality-duty-psed-review-and-government-response. Accessed 14 Dec 2018.

Lewis, H. (2019, March 15). *Interview Between the Author and Huw Lewis, Customer Services Director of NEXUS.*

NEXUS. (2018). *Hate Crime Charter for Public Transport.* Tyne and Wear: NEXUS. Online at: https://www.nexus.org.uk/sites/default/files/hate_crime_charter_for_public_transport.pdf. Accessed 17 Dec 2018.

Nottingham Express Transit. (2018). *Email Response to Researcher 27/06/2018.* Nottingham: Nottingham Express Transit.

Office of Rail and Road (ORR). (2018). *Disabled Persons Protection Policy.* Online at: http://orr.gov.uk/rail/licensing/licensing-the-railway/disabled-peoples-protection-policy. Accessed 24 Dec 2018.

Stop Hate UK. (2017a). *Stop Hate UK Website*. Online at: http://www.stophateuk.org/. Accessed 15 Dec 2018.

Stop Hate UK. (2017b, August 7). *Email from 'Mike' Representing Stop Hate UK to the Author Regarding Training Structure*.

Transport for London (TfL). (2017, August 14). *Interview Between the TfL Operational Standards Team Representative and the Author*.

Virgin Trains East Coast (VTEC) (now renamed London North Easter Railways). (2018). *Email Response from Customer Service Team VTN-180116BRRZ Received on 1st March 2018*. York: Virgin Trains East Coast.

CHAPTER 6

Disability Hate Crime: What Did We Already Know, What Is New?

Abstract This chapter takes the data revealed in Chaps. 3, 4 and 5 and aligns it with established academic research. The objective here is to ascertain if the experiences of victims and the behaviours of abusers broadly align with that in founded research studies. Aside from focusing on the techniques of abuse and the shorter- and longer-term impacts of abuse, the chapter will additionally explore the acts of collaboration and bystander non-intervention which have been revealed through my research. As well as established research, this chapter will disclose a new explanatory framework to explicate why previously unoffending fellow passengers collaborate in the abuse of disabled people. Collaborative Alimentation Theory is, in itself, new, although it is built on the shoulders of established theorisation.

Keywords Established literature • Explanatory framework of collaboration • Bystander non-intervention • Theories of crime • Why people collaborate to abuse

6.1 Chapter Introduction

This book has gathered evidence from victims of disability hate crime on public transport and outlined the current legislative position in the UK concerning the Public Sector Equality Duty. The statute makes the promoting and reporting of equality, and the associated duty of care, the

D. Wilkin, *Disability Hate Crime*, Palgrave Hate Studies,
https://doi.org/10.1007/978-3-030-28726-9_6

responsibility of authorities and those contracted by those authorities to provide public transport, among other public services. All public agencies and service providers are encumbered with the same general duty when conducting, arranging or contracting the provision of public services. My research has found that some passengers face repeated hostility on public transport due to their disability and that duties to protect the equalities of disabled people are not, in the main, being enacted or enforced by either public transport authorities or service providers.

This chapter will thematically synthesise literature, theory and law and will also look towards future policy direction. The purpose of this chapter is to consolidate evidence and prepare an argument for enhancing the safeguarding of the travelling public on UK public transport. The chapter will therefore capture the essence of the findings from my research which were presented in Chaps. 3, 4 and 5 and discuss these alongside established academic knowledge. Additionally, this chapter will extend knowledge by offering a new theory as an explanatory framework to explicate some elements of offender behaviour. That theory concerns observations of collaborative alienation—the term which I have applied to the behaviour where attempts were made to recruit previously unoffending passengers in the abusive attacks. Having consolidated the evidence, going forward, Chap. 7 will delineate specific recommendations to improve the safeguarding of disabled and non-disabled public transport passengers alike.

6.2 Themes from Findings

When policy decisions are considered, one of the sources of information for any debate is often academic evidence gathered through rigorous research studies which is then reviewed by peers and then published. The established academic literature in the hate crime field cites the propensity for long-term fear and social isolation caused by repeated episodes of abuse and humiliation. Whether these attacks are established to maintain hegemonies of power (e.g., see Perry 2009) or are opportunist incarnations of attacker frustrations which manifest themselves in outpourings of hate (e.g., see Iganski 2008), the effect on the victim is the same. The outcomes of hate attacks are magnified by the personal nature of the abuse. As I am fully aware, this deconstruction of the victim's identity has the potential to cause enhanced and prolonged psychological problems. Despite many reports indicating that public transport is a known trigger environment for disability hate crime (Chakraborti et al. 2014; EHRC 2011; Home Office 2018), disabled people often continue to be victims of disability hate crime on UK public transport modes. For many disabled passengers using public transport, abuse and humiliation are everyday expectations. Abuse ranges from name-calling to psychological and physical violence, serious assault and serious sexual assault. The distress of abuse has led to some disabled people withdrawing from using public transport and subsequently to social isolation and missed opportunities for education, health and employment (DfT 2018).

One catalyst for abuse is often a dispute concerning wheelchair spaces or priority seating and this was evident in 60% of cases revealed in my research. The majority of all abuse, some 80%, was found to be perpetrated on buses and trams. Discussion as to why this environment offers a higher risk for hostility will be discussed in Chap. 7. The principal offender in these hate attacks has been known to make use of formerly unoffending fellow passengers to predicate and exacerbate this abuse. In my research, participants reported this phenomenon in 71% of incidents on buses and trams and in 23% of incidents on trains totalling 354 coded attributions with 52% of participants experiencing this effect overall. Fellow passengers, aside from those collaborating with the principal offender, mainly chose to ignore the victim's plight during and after the abuse even when the victim was clearly upset. In a situation where victims may look towards figures in authority to help them in their distress, it is poignant to note that also staff members were either unwilling or unable to help manage these situations and report the outcomes. Both victim participants and public transport staff thought that this may be due to insufficient or ineffective staff training.

6.3 Setting the Research Outcomes Against Established Academic Evidence

The everyday nature of experiences of hostility was brought to light by many participants in my study. For example:

> *I was on the tram and her usual trick was to humiliate me for being on benefits. She used to say things like: are you still on benefits, are you still claiming, how much do you get? For all those years and I was humiliated every time I went on the tram for about ten years. All the time, all the time, on an on and on.*

This is similar to the type of continuing and consistent humiliation and unendurable behaviour which Quarmby brought to our attention as long ago as 2008 (Quarmby 2008). This type of hostility, Quarmby argues, remains mainly unnoticed in public discourse where it becomes publicly acceptable. This behaviour has not generally attracted the vociferousness of either academics or those venturing to exploit identity politics in the UK. The latter implies that it has remained in an unexplored discursive silo by politicians who cannot see the issue as a popular vote-winner (Mason-Bish 2010; Roulstone and Mason-Bish 2013). Nevertheless, it remains very real and frightening to those who suffer its ravages on a daily basis. With the World Health Organisation estimating that as many as 15–19% of the world's population being disabled at any one time, it is reasonable to infer that the potential for suffering disability hate crime can only be proportionate to this figure (World Health Organisation (WHO) 2017). Add to this, the potential that disabled people might have as much as a 1.5 times higher chance of being victims of violence and abuse; then the chance of being abused on public transport magnifies (Hughes et al. 2012). Furthermore, data illustrates that hate crime on public transport has been on a continually rising trend since September 2005. Although this may be as a consequence of improved reporting pathways, it remains symbolic of a troubling continual increase in hostility towards disabled people (British Transport Police 2015, 2016, 2017a, b). This supposedly unnoticeable crime is exemplified here:

> *I take it as read that I'm going to have a shit journey. And nobody cares if I get a slating [abused], or not. People don't care. I don't blame them, why should they—but they have better things to do than worry about a cripple.*

The *ordinariness* of these crimes may be seated in perceptions of social acceptability. The perpetration of disability hate crime may not be causally linked to subcultural or right-wing group activity but could instead be couched in the overflowing feelings of everyday *normal* travellers. These travellers might feel resentment for the disabled person or harbour feelings that these people are *scroungers* who do not add value to society (Aiden and McCarthy 2014; Chakraborti and Garland 2012; Hollomotz 2013a; Walters 2011). Alternatively, outbursts might represent a failure to practise self-control which could stem from poor parenting. As Walters (2011) argued, self-control thresholds may be the deciding factor between maintaining a respectful silence and venting hurtful feelings on another person.

The ordinariness of these episodes of hostility, bullying, offensiveness and psychological torture in my study is generally sympathetic to those found in the large scale 2014 research of Chakraborti et al. (2014). The abuse was not perhaps *outrageous* in the public context, but almost at a level it was taken for granted and expected. In further accord with that study, my research found that victims declare acceptance of these abusive episodes and soon give up any thoughts of retaliation to the hateful confrontations which they are forced to endure day after day. Hollomotz (2013a) argued that this everyday offensiveness is a manifestation of power imbalances, which in my research are played out in the bus or the train. The offender sees the potential victim as weaker, susceptible and unlikely to be supported by fellow passengers (Reynald 2010):

> *I had been shopping and feeling so tired because the lifts didn't work. I had to ask others to help, which is embarrassing anyway. Then this guy started telling the other bus passengers that disabled people are a joke and that we are useless and 'get in the fucking way'. The others started laughing and that's when it got really scary. He said 'they take-up room, stink, wipe their shit everywhere and cost us money…'.*

Hollomotz (2013a) asserted that the disabled victim is less likely to have friends or influential acquaintances and is therefore less inclined to seek help or advice, and these characteristics help to make that person a prospective victim. Furthermore, the disabled victim is statistically less likely to report the offence or to chase the offender; characteristics which align with Routine Activity Theory (Felson 2002; Iganski 2008). Routine Activity Theory espouses that given the lowered capability of effective guardianship and thus an increased opportunity for successful offending, an attack is therefore is more viable for the perpetrator. There may of course be other reasons for offenders wanting to cause discomfort to a disabled victim. McDevitt et al. (2002) would argue through their typology of offending that offenders may be defending *normality*, as they see it, or being on a mission to erase disabled people from society generally or from that mode of transport specifically. Alternatively, they may just be thrill-seeking or sending a message that other disabled people are not welcome in that place. An example of being unwelcome follows:

> *I was moving toward [getting on] the bus but the ramp was still not lowered. The door was open so I asked if she would lower the ramp. She turned to me and told me that I was a 'fucking nuisance'—she did it quietly so that other*

passengers would not hear this. But then she turned to those passengers and said, quite clearly 'she's got to come on. It will slow us right down but don't blame me blame her'. I was being made a freak. Others laughed; some were patient and looked sympathetic. But one bloke said to his mate that 'we're all fucked now'. Do you know how I felt? Do you know what that feels like?

In my findings, participants also told of their stigmatisation on social media, being groundlessly portrayed as paedophiles or as *evil* people. This type of stigmatisation was cited by Quarmby in 2008 as one of the weapons of hatred which are deployed against disabled people, weapons which continue to be deployed (Quarmby 2008). Furthermore, not only do disabled passengers face abuse from offenders on a regular basis but they are also further humiliated by formerly unoffending passengers joining forces with the offender to exacerbate the negative experience of the victim. Disabled victims can look to fellow passengers for support and sympathy. When they do not receive this, it is not only disappointing but also leaves the victim feeling alone and unwanted. Moreover, when those potential allies turn against the victim in a concerted abusive episode, then participants feel bitterly let down and unrecognised:

For ten long minutes everyone on the lower deck listened to a public shaming of my body my life and my worth. And then it followed, the total silence that left me more exposed and isolated than any of the vitriol that had been directed at me. I desperately needed someone on that bus to acknowledge what had taken place – that didn't happen.

…

On the bus I felt incapacitated, in part, by the inaction of my fellow passengers

…

I didn't need them to know exactly what to do to help. But I did want them to be present and to acknowledge what was happening to me.

…

No one else spoke at all; there must have been 20 people downstairs on the bus.

Do you know it's funny. They find something in the newspaper which they had not seen before. Something so fascinating that they must read it at that moment.

My work is also in harmony with that of Walters et al. (2016), in noting that some participants see the use of public transport as a necessary evil, one which has to be endured because life has to go on. However, not every participant to my study could cope in this way and many were forced to stay at home where they feel safe and in a place where they would not be stressed or ridiculed. For these people, the prospect of yet another battle against abuse, is one experience too many. It was easier therefore to remain isolated. Many participants voiced their absolute weakness, both in physical and psychological terms, of being unable to have the strength to face another barrage of abuse, or if they did face one, too weak to do anything about it. They felt unable to retaliate, unable to report it and unable to cope with any more humiliation. The tiredness which invaded the lives of participants during their daily situation was palpable when participants were relating their evidence to me. This acceptance and impassiveness is firmly in accord with research by Iganski and Lagou (2015) who argued that these abuses become routine. Participants of my study did, in some cases, develop anti-abuse coping mechanisms. Accepting the abuse, ignoring the offender, and using humour to self-humiliate and take the stress out of their situation were all mentioned as coping strategies. These become important life skills:

> *… [I] bite my tongue …*

If any are taken, immediate actions by victims were mainly passive. Victims rarely showed any inclination towards retaliation, argument or for any verbal defence of their predicament. The following examples of immediate actions were widely representative of the participant cohort:

> *People heard this interaction and it drew attention to me and it made me feel as if I didn't have the right to ask for this seat so I'm very aware of going home and getting this negative reaction again so it makes me extremely anxious.*
>
> *I had been shopping and was feeling weak. I simply didn't have the strength to argue with him. He walked away, smiling and nodding at the other passengers like he had scored a victory. Well, perhaps he had because he got a couple of appreciative nods too.*
>
> *I did get on and I did not say another thing to her I was just so shocked. I was just rattling.*

Otherwise, there were passive examples from participants. Here are examples:

> *I did make eye-contact with another passenger. I just shook my head and he smiled, a kind of understanding I guess. It was just recognition of what happened, not much, but something.*

Sometimes I stare at them, I just stare. They then either stop looking at me or stare straight back. That's when it can get dangerous.

Although rare, some victims were found to have made a vociferous defence of their situation; these are examples of when participants reached their breaking point. It is interesting to note that in these cases, the attackers suppressed any further abuse:

… they are always loud always provoking you everything is 'f'In' and 'c…' they want you to be notice … Makes them look good. If you bang into them they think hang on a minute this old boy might give me some …

This was the final straw. I said 'you are not manhandling me like a piece of meat you can fuck off'. Terrible really (laughing). He said "but you are delaying us".

…

I said that if nobody turns-up then I would have to press the alarm button. That really made me popular – there were sighs and 'oh God's' all round at that.

I'm not a shrinking violet, you know? I can stand on my own steam.

Victims did report incidents. These reports sometimes brought retaliation against victims for having revealed hate crimes and incidents. Here are examples:

We ended-up doing a stupid thing we got the paper involved The XXX (local newspaper). And of course they wanted a picture and we got beat up for it because we told the paper.

He followed me. Once he jumped out in front of me with a stupid mask on. He gave me the middle finger and ran off. He must lead a boring life. He never forgave me for telling the police.

Indeed, Clement et al. (2011) drawing on an earlier survey from Thornicroft et al. (2009) worked with people with schizophrenia. Their study found that many people with mental health issues fear being further stigmatised and magnifying their victimisation if they reported being victims of abuse. The research of Clement et al. also found that people with mental health issues prefer to be less noticeable than other people and therefore avoid defending themselves or reporting victimisation for fear that they will be brought into the limelight and thus potentially attracting further stigmatisation. Moreover, Chakraborti et al. (2014) revealed that 41% of the perpetrators of disability hate crimes were personally known to the victims and these relationships clearly exacerbate any opportunity for retaliation following reporting an incident. Additional data from the Chakraborti et al. study indicates that 75% of offending involves more than one offender and that 72% of offenders are under 30 years of age. These data arguably make retaliation and reporting less likely to occur; if, for example, the victim is being intimidated by a group of younger people, they may be less likely to want to attract further abuse. In other words, the size and age profile of that group might dissuade the victim from reporting the issue. Disabled people may also be dissuaded from reporting incidents and have reduced capacity to defend themselves because of their experience of receiving disrespect and even abuse from healthcare staff and other figures in authority. A report sponsored by a charity for mental disability in the UK, Scope, revealed this (Aiden and McCarthy 2014). Aiden and McCarthy found that 23% of disabled people in their study would appreciate an improvement in the attitudes of the very people who were tasked with caring for their needs—the professionals with whom they had the most contact. This effect, and the propensity for disabled people to be at a higher risk of abuse from those who are designated to care for them in the form of friends and family, could create the capacity for the disabled victim not to place trust in professionals generally. This distrust may result in them not wanting to report anything through them. The argument of Iganski and Lagou (2015), using empirical data from the Crime Survey of England and Wales, supports this aversion to report crime. They found that while people with a disability are more likely to endure long-term negative psychological effects from hate crime, they are also less likely to report these actions.

Aside from the short-term and immediate impacts of hate offences, Iganski and Lagou (2015) also contribute to the discussion of longer-term effects. Their study emphasises that 41% of hate crime victims are more likely to be 'very much' emotionally affected by hate crime in the long-term than a comparative 18% of victims suffering non-hate crime (2015:41). Of these, crimes against the person have more than double the impact when compared against non-hate crime. Iganski and Lagou argued that fear, depression and anxiety are common outcomes of hate crime which are more likely to result in behavioural changes or moving residence than non-hate crimes might:

I don't tend to think about what happens immediately after. But having said that, I it might just hit me a few weeks or months later. I'd be doing something quite ordinary like sleeping or something. Then suddenly, you know what I

> *mean, you just get shit. The whole shit comes in to your mind in a flood and without warning, all the details and everything. I don't know what brings it on. My way of getting over it is to start shouting. Not at anyone in particular—but just replaying the situation with me as the hero this time. I give them hell! I tell them what I think of them and how fucking useless they are as human beings. My finger wags as well ... I suppose it's sad really because I don't say any of this to their faces. It makes me feel better though. But it's nowhere near to getting justice I suppose.*

These longer-term impacts of abuse might include isolating themselves from social activity and avoiding leaving their homes. They are additionally at risk of fear from crime enacted locally against disabled people which act as signal crimes. Signal, or message, crimes act to increase perceptions of future victimisation and disabled people are susceptible to this dear whether, or not, these crimes were actually intended as signal crimes (Paterson et al. 2018; Perry 2003). The EHRC (2011) report emphasised a propensity for disabled people to suffer from fear and a loss of self-confidence and that these were the restrictive outcomes of hostility towards disabled people. Furthermore, people with mental health issues are especially susceptible to social isolation (Clement et al. 2011). This isolation is likely to affect access to work and to educational facilities and lead to restrictions regarding the use of leisure and recreational facilities (Office for National Statistics [ONS] 2015). These restrictions will therefore limit the ability to develop, to work and to enjoy life, in other words to be isolated from the lifestyles which non-disabled people enjoy:

> *I avoid using the trams now. I talk funny and I get hurt for it. I don't like being hurt. It hurts me. I don't go no more.*

The effect of social isolation and restricted lifestyle activity is not limited to the victim themselves. Beadle-Brown et al. (2014) and a related academic piece (Richardson et al. 2016) both disclosed the amount and types of victimisation suffered by people with autism alongside their caregivers, family and friends. These studies cite the *ripple effect* which secondary victims could be prone to. These studies revealed emotional outbursts from the primary victim at the frustration of being at home for extended periods or associates suffering the backlash from the primary victim failing to cope with being the target of hostility. Additionally, if the victim is personally known to the perpetrator, that perpetrator might visit the home of the disabled person to continue the abuse causing stress to all living there.

Participants of the Beadle-Brown et al. (2014) report described having windows broken and they themselves being victims of with, or without, the presence of the disabled person for whom they care. The extent of the abuse suffered by the primary victim can extend over long periods and has included being spat at, bullying and physical violence (Mind 2007). Any attempt to complain to the police or other authorities has evidently led to extended periods of stress and concern. The difficulty in not being believed in the first place is further exacerbated by the bureaucratic process which follows and the stress of awaiting a decision from the Crown Prosecution Service which could potentially take months to process. During this time, the pressures of engaging in official and legal correspondence, the family pressures of not knowing how the process will change their lifestyles and the potential for continued victimisation permeate the lives of the victim, their family and friends. Participants of my study gave examples of their experiences of social isolation. Some of these follow:

> *I don't go out – I don't like going out at all. As you know from my email this video of me was posted on the internet (Facebook) and it was later taken down when I complained to them but by then the damage had been done.*
>
> *Why me? I felt why did they all want me to suffer? What had I done to them? What could I do to them? Why would I want to come out of my place if this is all I get for doing it? Why can't they leave me alone? [Crying].*
>
> *You lose the confidence to face every day things and situations.*
>
> …
>
> *I hate it! I cry! I have nightmares about being trapped on a bus with these idiots!*

The propensity for social disadvantage and the longer-term impacts of being abused are statistically linked to being unemployed, educationally disadvantaged and isolated as well as to having a *transport disadvantage* (Delbosc and Currie 2011). A transport disadvantage in this context relates to not having one's own means of transport and needing to rely on public transport provision. This reliance also makes some people *'transit captives'* (Sung-suk et al. 2014:197). However, as has been gathered from the participant cohort to my study, many victims of abuse on public transport also share a reticence to use those services in the future. Here are some examples:

> *I think that we have both been insulted and if that is the level of intellect that we are to expect on public transport then we would be better-off keeping away from it and not using it.*

> *... and it does make a difference I do choose to stay in more and I do have commitments but I can't face them because of how I'm treated on the bus sometimes. I had committed to something and at the last minute I say no. because if I have two buses and a Tube either way that's six chances for something to go wrong and that's too much to bear.*
>
> *It's been horrendous and I don't know how many years we've been trying to do something about it. So we don't bother now with the buses not if we can possibly help it.*
>
> ...
>
> *That's why we have stopped using the buses – we just get a taxi.*
>
> ...
>
> *... Oh no we're not bothering; we just keep ourselves to ourselves now.*

The Papworth Trust asserted that 42% of people with disabilities are over the UK state pension age and that 57% of disabilities involve mobility problems (Papworth Trust 2016). These factors further contribute to result in those people with a transport disadvantage (Delbosc and Currie 2011) enduring a huge encumbrance every time that they leave their residence, let alone travel to a different area. Therefore, good quality, safe and reliable public transport is an essential element of everyday life for many disabled people. Any reluctance to use these services can only result in isolation, lifestyle restriction and reduced opportunities to enjoy life. Align this with the mind statistics that 71% of disabled people had been victimised, which rises to 90% in areas of social housing, and that 18% of disabled people only really feel safe when they are in their own homes and it might become easier to understand why so many disabled people lose faith in public transport (Mind 2007). Public transport has been widely reported as being a known trigger environment for hostility and hate offences against people with disabilities (Chakraborti et al. 2014; EHRC 2011; Home Office 2018). That the risk of crime is increased when using public transport is established (Beecroft and Pangbourne 2014). Add to these factors, the risk of being publicly filmed and the potential for those images to be placed on social media and the threats posed by public travel can be visualised (Quarmby 2008). Vilalta (2011) argued that there is a direct link between reducing the feeling of fear of using public transport and increased ridership especially in, or through, problematic neighbourhoods. Newton (2008) expands on the increased risk of susceptibility concerning the route geography of some bus routes, the infrastructure in those areas and the associated crime rates. Newton argued that the environment through which the bus travels has a direct effect on fear perceived by the passenger. In light of the already extant fear of travel by the disabled passenger, therefore, this may be exacerbated by the route required to be taken (Hine 2007). Any reduction of such fear, Vilalta (2011) adds, would result in a better quality of lifestyle for those who need to use such modes of transport. In summarising this section, the burden of leaving the home, the physical struggle to use public transport, the fear of crime and the risk of abuse contribute to making a considered choice not to use public transport. Hodgson and Turner (2003) argued that not enough research exists either to help to understand exclusion from public transport or to drive any future action. Therefore, the chances of disabled people becoming more trustworthy of public transport seem remote in the near future.

To this point in the chapter, evidence has illustrated the everyday nature of the abuse which is suffered by victims of disability hate crime on public transport in the UK. The chapter then examined the immediate actions and the short-term impacts of victims before looking at the longer-term impacts and an associated reluctance to use public transport. This chapter has linked academic evidence to participant evidence from my study, and these seem to broadly harmonise. This chapter will now turn from linking participant evidence from established academic literature to emergent theorisation.

6.4 Collaborative Alienation

This section will discuss and substantiate the emergent phenomenon which became apparent when I was gathering witness and victim data for my research. This is the phenomenon around which I have developed an explanatory framework and which I have characterised as Collaborative Alienation Theory. Although this is a newly expounded theory, it rests squarely upon established criminological theories, whilst differing from others. The emergent behaviour, which was noticeable in 71% of incidents on buses and 23% of incidents on trains, was experienced by 52% of victims as recorded in 352 coded attributions throughout my study (for cited findings, see Chap. 3). This emergent theorisation was made possible by using grounded theory as the tool of analysis. Collaborative Alienation Theory explains situations in which the initial perpetrator makes allies of previously uninvolved passengers to predicate hostility against individuals. Three possible outcomes of these recruitment attempts were noted: successful recruitment where the new ally provides support to the principal offender; oppositional, where the potential recruit defends the victim; and ignorance, where the potential recruit evades engaging with the abusive situation altogether. This is dissimilar from McDevitt et al. (2002) typology where all members are enrolled prior to acts of perpetration. In Collaborative Alienation Theory, the principal offender seemingly uses a range of techniques to extemporaneously ally formerly unacquainted fellow passengers in his/her cause to alienate the hate crime victim. Their combined actions amount to this collaborative alienation. This is facilitated by the perpetrator in that she/he leads their fellow passengers, the *collaborators*, in an activity which they might otherwise not have participated in. *Alienation*, because the aim of the perpetrator is to be hostile toward, alienate or isolate the victim because of their difference and gain as much collaborative reinforcement as is possible.

Most cases of collaboration were recorded on buses and trams, and this may be a consequence of the restricted nature of these vehicles producing an inability to move to another area and escape any abuse or perhaps the restricted ability for allies also to move away. The absence of screening or compartmentation within buses may be the cause, and this may also result in the principal offender *controlling* potential recruits more easily. Without compartmentation, the abuser may be able to communicate widely across the bus or tram. Perhaps buses on short-haul routes generally utilising lower seat backs might also contribute to more easily facilitating control for the principal offender and again easing communication. For the principal offender using bus-based abuse, it might be easier for them to conduct collaborative alienation hostility as neither the victim nor their allies are able to escape the immediate area in-between bus stops. The victim could be trapped or unwilling to alight as this would result in having to wait for another bus. Moreover, the victim, if they have mobility issues, might be restricted to one area or seat. For obvious reasons, such collaborative alienation is unlikely to occur in a taxi unless more than one passenger is embarked and two of the occupants collaborate against the third. Although this type of collaboration has been evidenced on trains, this seems only to occur if the victim has restricted mobility. Wheelchair spaces offer little opportunity to move further around the train accept to use the toilet which is wheelchair-compatible and must be within easy reach of the dedicated wheelchair space to be compliant under the Rail Vehicle Accessibility (Non-Interoperable Rail System) Regulations 2010 (RVAR10). This example illustrates being a captive victim:

> *I was telling all the other passengers that I couldn't go anywhere until I got help to alight. I was trying to explain my situation. Then a man came along, he was looking out of the train for me and said that nobody was coming to help.*
>
> ...
>
> *Then another man loudly said to anyone who could hear 'we can't wait here forever'.*
>
> ...
>
> *... another guy came up and said that I was making everybody late—he was saying this so loudly and looking for support so that everyone would blame me.*
>
> ...
>
> *That was followed by cheers and yells from other passengers. This arrogant woman in a very expensive and tailored suit said that they should 'tip me on to the platform'. There was more laughing. I was so scared.*

Therefore, the restricted nature of this space potentially makes non-ambulant disabled persons effectively trapped.

Another potential benefit for a collaborator is that perhaps little chance for any continued involvement following the episode of abuse. The relationship between the perpetrator and the new allies seems to be instrumental and short-term. Alighting from the vehicle terminates the involvement of the ally and therefore the relationship between them and the perpetrator as well as the victim and the perpetrator. If the perpetrator is known to the victim or even accompanying them, hostilities can be suspended until the next time when the perpetrator once again has a bus audience to perform toward. There is little chance of recrimination as the perpetrator, any staff member, the allies or the victims are potentially unlikely to meet again. Moreover, there is, statistically perhaps, little chance that any hostility will be reported (Quarmby 2008). The benefits for the principal offender are clear in that they receive support for their offending. For the collaborators, the benefit is to become part of an ingroup, part of a mission:

> *I've seen this happen on more than one occasion; the main bloke, the one who starts it, looks around for support. If it seems that the main bloke is doing quite well, then others join-in. once a few start then it's a free-for-all. It's as if they feel that they can operate in safety, without blame. It's like it all comes out, all of their frustrations at once.*

Whatever the reasons for the collaboration being facilitated mainly on bus services, these would need to be established via other, more focused research. There may also be a potential to utilise Collaborative Alienation Theory as a framework to analyse interactions in wider society.

On the part of the collaborator—the formerly unoffending passenger—there seems to be a willingness to capitulate with the principal offender to conduct abuse. Arguably, they might not risk undertaking this abuse if they were acting alone. Becker (2013) argued that this type of behaviour is an attack against deviancy on individuals and groups which are considered as outsiders. Becker argued that relationships are formed to produce what may be collectively considered as justified actions. These actions follow a social lay judgement of what is deviant. Becker couches his explanation of deviancy by typifying the human need to attribute anything which may contribute to lessening the chances of human survival. Becker argued that these attributions need to be labelled as deviant—including human disability. The concept of disability has long been linked to deviancy and to abnormality (Quarmby 2013). Becker's argument states that deviants do not necessarily need to have broken any rules to be labelled thus. They do not need to have broken conventions, law or accepted practice. All they need to be, Becker argued, is an *outsider* to be labelled as deviant (Becker 2013:260; Allport 1954). What is however important is that boundaries are set between the *ingroup* and the *outgroup* to demarcate and legitimise the victimisation. These boundaries need to be protected to support power relationships whilst denigrating the victim group (Craig 2002; Perry 2003). Kunstman et al. (2013) cite through their meta-analysis that over ten years of research has yet to discern why people choose to be in a particular ingroup—and contrive to alienate outgroup members. But their work finds that there is a seemingly implicit need to be a part of a group and that recruitment is not in itself difficult. Furthermore, Vaes et al. (2012) argued that a process of dehumanisation is important in the demarcation of the ingroup/outgroup boundary. Any reduction of the outgroup to the status of being less than human will assist in the coagulating process which brings the ingroup together in this temporary and instrumental relationship. The following examples illustrate this:

> *Yes. That's what I thought, bloody cheek! He was doing this to make the crowd on the platform laugh – but I considered this really insulting.*
>
> *I've had the [principal] abuser say that I was "blocking the aisle" and that "if there was a fire then we would all be dead". Then I would be "done for murder". I remember just shaking my head but then somebody else chimed-in and called me a "selfish bitch".*

The opportunistic nature of Routine Activity Theory additionally contributes to an understanding of Collaborative Alienation Theory by emphasising that if conditions are appropriate, then opportunistic crime is more likely to occur (Felson 2002; Iganski 2008). Routine Activity Theory asserts that if the chance to commit a crime occurs then an opportunist offender might exploit this, provided that capable guardianship of the victim is in a lowered state—in other words, the victim seems susceptible to attack. As Iganski (2008) argued, hate offending might, or might not, be primary motivation but that the offender just ceases the chance to vent their feelings. However, of course this does not preclude these aggressions from being determined as hate incidents and offences under current legislation:

> *… she just looked straight ahead and said nothing. I tackled her and said … you would make me wait for the next bus just in case you might wake your baby? She then started screaming at me … calling me a parasite [abuse] blaming me for living on benefits [justification]. She was not talking to me though, but to others. I was in tears and everybody was looking at me. I was in the middle of the aisle and I was crying*
>
> …

It may be that if the principal offender uses a routine opportunity to do this, then why should this attitude not be embraced by fellow passengers who might be willing to be recruited to assist in that offending. The crowded nature of the vehicle might improve the opportunity to offend (Newton and Ceccato 2015; Purifoye 2015). Moreover, research by Reynald (2010) states that capable guardianship is a critical element in the perpetrator deciding to commit an offence. Reynald argued that the capability and expertise of guardianship is enhanced by the potential victim feeling comfortable and familiar with their environment. In other words, the more familiar with their surroundings that they are, the more likely the victim is to feel able to protect themselves. Public transport is, by its nature, an ever-changing place where strangers come and go. Therefore, there is seemingly little chance that the victim will be able to feel comfortable in an environment which is constantly in a state of change.

Hollomotz (2013b) adds credence to this line of theorisation by arguing that power imbalance through a perceived *vulnerability* makes the disabled person a viable target for opportunist abuse. An implicit social understanding that the disabled person is less likely to form friendships and less likely to report crime added to a propensity towards weakness might limit their motivation to defend themselves. This perceived vulnerability added to the opportunity to vent prejudice might constitute a powerful formula to set the scene for abusive offending. Adding to power imbalance theorisation, Perry (2003) argued that socially constructed dualisms are inherent in society and demarcate acceptable practices, individuals and groups from the *other*, the unacceptable, and the unwelcome. It is the role of the accepted group, Perry argued, to *police* the boundaries between their group and the Other (Perry 2003:98). In doing so this maintains hegemonic superiority over inferior groups. Perry further argued that 'these structures of power and oppression permeate society' to ensure that power remains with the oppressors and that their identity must be 'established and re-established in varied conditions' to maintain superiority (2003:100–3). Moreover, when subordinate groups try to threaten this superiority, for example, by disabled people establishing a dominant or privileged status on public transport, then that threat 'must be repressed' (2003:104).

As well as outgroup demarcation, dehumanisation and a potential for routine activities, techniques of neutralisation seem to be prevalent in the behaviours around the instrumental victimisation which results in collaborative alienation. Hopkins Burke (2014, drawing on Matza 1964) argued that people plagued by doubt around their own acceptance in society, masculinity and adulthood are willing to capitulate to ingroup practices to authenticate their own individual identities. This process leaves group members 'trapped in a vicious circle of mutual misunderstanding' Hopkins Burke argued (2014:154). This process, which Matza sees as an, albeit temporary, drift into deviancy, is assisted by techniques of neutralisation. These techniques involve group members justifying and legitimising their actions by neutralising the humanisation, feelings and rights of outgroup members. In doing so, they provide vindications for their actions. Some of the principal acts of denial which ingroup members might potentially utilise during Collaborative Alienation are:

1. Denial of responsibility (I didn't mean it)
2. Denial of injury (I didn't really harm him)
3. Denial of the Victim (he deserved it)
4. Condemnation of the condemners (they always pick on us). (Hopkins Burke 2014:154; Sykes and Matza 1957)

These tools of defining the outgroup, dehumanising the victim and neutralising the consequences are the building blocks of Collaborative Alienation Theory. Although some of the supportive theories above may have been written specifically with youth and deviance in mind, many of the elements of these theories seem to add weight to Collaborative Alienation Theory. An example from my study of dehumanisation follows:

> *But they said well "we have priority over you". I said how is that then? He said "nobody queues these days". Anyway, I managed to get on and then they started – not swearing – but giving jibes about being in a wheelchair and "taking up three seat places". I said sorry but where can I go. They said, well "get off and wait for another bus".*

This however leaves academia asking why bystanders fail to intervene when obvious victimisation is occurring. Why do those who were not recruited to become collaborators of the principal offender fail to take an opposing view or do anything to intervene and choose instead to ignore the situation? This is partially addressed by understanding the dynamics of the outgroup. Although not wanting to be an active member of the ingroup, formerly unoffending passengers may not want to commit themselves as far as being identified as members of the abused outgroup; in other words siding with the disabled victim. This could have the result of making themselves victims of the principal offender and of any collaborators which that offender may manage to recruit. Whilst not wishing harm upon the victim, they will not go as far as siding with them and potentially incurring the wrath of the abusers. An examination of why bystanders do not get involved to ameliorate these situations of hostility was outside of the scope of my research but is certainly necessary: this may be due to a fear of harm to themselves, a fear of misunderstanding the situation, not wanting to look foolish or perhaps a feeling that the situation is not of their making or indeed any of their business. They may, of course, sympathise with the abuse without wanting to commit to assisting the offender(s). Established theorisation concerning bystander non-intervention is provided by Cohen (1993). Cohen argued that bystanders face a dilemma when witnessing victimisation. The prototype for bystander non-intervention, Cohen argued, is the Kitty Genovese case in New York during 1964. Kitty was assaulted in a busy street for over 40 minutes and at least 38 witnesses saw this happening but did nothing to either intervene or to call for assistance.

Kitty died as a result of that assault. Research by Sheleff (1978, cited in Cohen 1993) suggested the following three explanations for non-intervention:

1. Diffusion of responsibility (why should I intervene?)
2. Inability to identify the victim (we help our family, friends or ingroup, we do not help those not in our 'universe')
3. Inability to conceive an effective intervention (what should I do?). (Sheleff, 1978 cited in Cohen 1993:656)

Furthermore, Reynald (2010) conducted empirical research to understand why bystanders decline to become involved in crime deterrence. Reynald's research focused on low-, medium- and high-crime areas and the propensity of bystanders to intervene. Reynald finds that bystanders are generally successful in deterring crime once they do decide to become involved. Indeed, Reynald's research found that most bystanders are willing to take some type of action. This action however may be simply monitoring the evolving situation or reporting it to a third party whilst not becoming directly involved themselves. Reynald additionally found that in high-crime areas, the bystander was only half as likely to want to become involved. Other factors in the decision to intervene included the size and perceived physical characteristics of the assailant and the personal safety of the bystander. Participants of the Reynald study also stated that their propensity to intervene would be increased if family members were the intended targets of the crime. Some examples of bystander non-intervention from my study follow:

> *On the bus I felt incapacitated, in part, by the inaction of my fellow passengers. Even the guy that offered the seat just sat back in it as if nothing had happened.*

To offset a critique of Collaborative Alienation Theory, the theories cited in relation to the illustration of the effects of the abuse of disabled people on public transport are established theories from academic, peer-reviewed sources. These are used in synthesis with the evidence gathered from the interviewees and focus groups used within my research which were collected within the parameters set by the methodologies set out in Chap. 2. The victim-participant cohort for the interviews and focus groups numbered 56 in total. Therefore, my research offers a substantial participant contribution which has been aligned with established academic peer-reviewed research. This makes these sections of the chapter robust in their explanation of participant experience in its alignment with established academic work. Collaborative Alienation Theory is itself underpinned by four established theories and is synthesised with participant experience. It developed entirely as a grounded theory, directly from participant data. The original questioning which I utilised did not initially contemplate the emergence of this theory but questioning began to reveal the existence of the new theory, and subsequently, questioning was adjusted to explore this further.

Some challenges to this theorisation might cite the size of the participant cohort and the strength of the emergent theory. The cohort is relatively sizable in academic terms—and 52% of participants did relate aspects of the emergent theory as phenomena which they had personally experienced. Clearly however, a larger cohort focusing directly on this emergent theory would continue to strengthen veracity. My research was not established to focus on this as a particular phenomenon but the research techniques used in the study have legitimised the use of grounded theory to draw it out. However, it should be noted that until Collaborative Alienation Theory is fully tested, its robustness will remain in question. Questions arising out of emergent theorisation will be posed in the conclusion, Chap. 7. Any critique of this theory might indicate that it was weak in offering an explanation as to why the offender would wish to recruit others to help perpetrate the offending or why a formerly unoffending passenger would want to contribute. For answers to these dilemmas, the offenders and collaborators would need to be questioned regarding their motivations—and this work was outside of the scope of my research. However, this theorisation could lay the groundwork for future, more specific, research.

To summarise, this section has introduced the Collaborative Alienation Theory as an explanatory framework. In doing so it has offered supportive academic theorisations which, in their separate parts, go towards substantiating collaborative alienation. Therefore, it may be prudent to ask why a new theory is being proposed at all. Its potential use nonetheless is in wider society, although this claim needs to be assessed. The theory has helped to understand the nuances of abusive actions which might translate to other social spaces. Further work is required however to understand why these formerly unoffending collaborators would choose to either accept or decline the opportunity to assist the principal offender.

6.5 Summary of Chapter 6

This chapter has provided a discussion following the findings from my research. The chapter related these data to peer-reviewed academic literature; in doing so, the areas of the everyday, the short-term impacts, the long-term effects and the reluctance to use public transport were discussed. Following this discussion, Collaborative Alienation Theory was introduced. The discovery of which justified the use of grounded theory in my research project. In the discussion, several themes were drawn together to signify the levels of abuse which people with disabilities face on public transport, almost on a daily basis. Moreover, the longer-term impacts of this abuse were behavioural change, social isolation, economic inactivity and educational deficits. The fear of travelling in public often overcame any necessity to travel. Clearly, if this situation does not improve and existing legislation remains not to be adhered to by public transport authorities and providers, then the daily experiences of disabled people using public transport are unlikely to change for the better. The result of this will undoubtedly be people continuing to isolate themselves from societal assets and from health and education provision. Furthermore, unless public transport staff members are better prepared to help—then they will remain unable to do so with any level of confidence. Chapter 7 will offer some direction towards future policy and recommendations to enhance the safety of disabled public transport users.

Bibliography

Aiden, H., & McCarthy, A. (2014). *Current Attitudes Towards Disabled People*. London: Scope.

Allport, G. (1954). *The Nature of Prejudice*. Cambridge, MA: Addison-Wesley.

Beadle-Brown, J., Richardson, L., Guest, C., Malovic, A., Bradshaw, J., & Himmerich, J. (2014). *Living in Fear: Better Outcomes for People with Learning Disabilities and Autism (Main Research Report)*. Canterbury: Tizard Centre, University of Kent.

Becker, H. (2013). Outsiders. In E. McLaughlin & J. Muncie (Eds.), *Criminological Perspectives* (3rd ed.). London: Sage.

Beecroft, M., & Pangbourne, K. (2014). Future Prospects for Personal Security in Travel by Public Transport. *Transportation Planning and Technology, 38*(1), 131–148.

British Transport Police (BTP). (2015). *Hate Crime Strategy 2015*. London: British Transport Police.

British Transport Police (BTP). (2016). *British Transport Police: We Stand Together Campaign Website*. London: British Transport Police. Online at: http://www.btp.police.uk/advice_and_information/how_we_tackle_crime/hate_crime.aspx. Accessed 2 Jan 2019.

British Transport Police (BTP). (2017a, August 3). *Interview Between the Author and Inspector Granville Sellers, Deputy Lead for Hate Crimes, of the BTP Safeguarding Hub*. Leeds: British Transport Police.

British Transport Police (BTP). (2017b). *British Transport Police: Crime Statistics*. London: British Transport Police. Online at: http://www.btp.police.uk/about_us/your_right_to_information/publications.aspx. Accessed 2 Jan 2019.

Chakraborti, N., & Garland, J. (2012). Reconceptualizing Hate Crime Victimisation Through the Lens of Vulnerability and 'Difference'. *Theoretical Criminology, 16*(4), 499–514.

Chakraborti, N., Garland, J., & Hardy, S.-J. (2014). *The Leicester Hate Crime Project: Findings and Conclusions*. Leicester: University of Leicester.

Clement, S., Brohan, E., Sayce, L., Pool, J., & Thornicroft, G. (2011). Disability Hate Crime, Targeted Violence and Hostility: A Mental Health and Discrimination Perspective. *Journal of Mental Health, 20*(3), 219–225.

Cohen, S. (1993). Human Rights and Crimes of State. In E. McLaughlin & J. Muncie (Eds.) (2013), *Criminological Perspectives* (3rd ed.). London: Sage.

Craig, K. (2002). Examining Hate- Motivated Aggression: A Review of the Social Psychological Literature on Hate Crimes as a Distinct Form of Aggression. *Aggression and Violent Behaviour, 7*(1), 85–101.

Delbosc, A., & Currie, G. (2011). Exploring the Relative Influences of Transport Disadvantage and Social Exclusion on Well-Being. *Transport Policy, 18*(4), 555–562.

Department for Transport. (2018). *The Inclusive Transport Strategy: Achieving Equal Access for Disabled People*. London: Department for Transport.

Equality and Human Rights Commission (EHRC). (2011). *Hidden in Plain Sight: Inquiry into Disability-Related Harassment*. Manchester: Equality and Human Rights Commission.

Felson, M. (2002). *Crime and Everyday Life* (3rd ed.). Thousand Oaks: Sage.

Hine, J. (2007). Transport Disadvantage and Social Exclusion in the UK. In G. Currie (Ed.), *No Way to Go Transport and Social Disadvantage in Australian Communities*. Clayton: Monash University ePress.

Hodgson, F., & Turner, J. (2003). Participation Not Consumption: The Need for New Participatory Practices to Address Transport and Social Exclusion. *Transport Policy, 10*(2003), 265–272.

Hollomotz, A. (2013a). Disability, Oppression and Violence: Towards a Sociological Explanation. *Sociology, 47*(3), 477–493.

Hollomotz, A. (2013b). Disability and the Continuum of Violence Crime. In A. Roulstone & H. Mason-Bish (Eds.), *Disability, Hate Crime and Violence*. Abingdon: Routledge.

Home Office. (2018). *Home Office: Hate Crime Statistics.* Online at: https://www.gov.uk/government/statistics/hate-crime-england-and-wales-2017-to-2018. Accessed 17 Dec 2018.

Hopkins Burke, R. (2014). *An Introduction to Criminological Theory* (4th ed.). Abingdon: Routledge.

Hughes, K., Bellis, M., Jones, L., Wood, S., Bates, G., Eckley, L., & Officer, A. (2012). Prevalence and Risk of Violence Against Adults with Disabilities: A Systematic Review and Meta-Analysis of Observational Studies. *Lancet, 379*, 1621–1629.

Iganski, P. (2008). *Hate Crime and the City.* Bristol: The Policy Press.

Iganski, P., & Lagou, S. (2015). The Personal Injuries of 'Hate Crime'. In N. Hall, A. Corb, & P. Giannasi (Eds.), *Routledge International Handbooks: Routledge International Handbook on Hate Crime* (pp. 34–46). New York: Routledge.

Kunstman, J., Plant, E., Zielaskowski, K., & Lacosse, J. (2013). Feeling in with the Outgroup: Outgroup Acceptance and the Internalization of the Motivation to Respond Without Prejudice. *Journal of Personality and Social Psychology, 105*(3), 443–457.

Mason-Bish, H. (2010). Future Challenges for Hate Crime Policy: Lessons from the Past. In N. Chakraborti (Ed.), *Hate Crime: Concepts, Policy, Future Directions* (pp. 58–77). Cullompton: Willan.

Matza, D. (1964). *Delinquency and Drift.* New York: Wiley.

McDevitt, J., Levin, J., & Bennett, S. (2002). Hate Crime Offenders: An Expanded Typology. *Journal of Social Issues, 58*(2), 303–317.

Mind. (2007). *Another Assault: Mind's Campaign for Equal Access to Justice for People with Mental Health Problems.* London: Mind.

Newton, A. (2008). A Study of Bus Route Crime Risk in Urban Areas: The Changing Environs of a Bus Journey, Built Environment (1978–). *Crime in the City, 34*(1), 88–103.

Newton, A., & Ceccato, V. (2015). Theoretical Perspectives of Security and Safety in Transit Environments. In V. Ceccato & A. Newton (Eds.), *Safety and Security in Transit Environments.* Basingstoke: Palgrave Macmillan.

Office for National Statistics. (2015). *Life Opportunities Survey: Third Wave 2015.* Online at: https://www.gov.uk/government/collections/life-opportunities-survey#history. Accessed 12 Dec 2018.

Papworth Trust. (2016). *Disability in the UK: Facts and Figures 2016.* Cambridge: The Papworth Trust.

Paterson, J., Walters, M., Brown, R., & Fearn, H. (2018). *The Sussex Hate Crime Project: Final Report.* Brighton: The University of Sussex.

Perry, B. (2003). Accounting for Hate Crime: Doing Difference. In B. Perry (Ed.), *Hate and Bias Crime: A Reader.* London: Routledge.

Perry, B. (Ed.). (2009). *Hate Crime* (Vol. 3). Westport: Praeger.

Purifoye, G. (2015). Nice-Nastiness and Other Raced Social Interactions on Public Transport Systems. *City & Community, 14*(3), 286–310.
Quarmby, K. (2008). *Getting Away with Murder: Disabled People's Experiences of Hate Crime in the UK*. London: Scope.
Quarmby, K. (2013). *Scapegoat: Why Are We Failing Disabled People*. London: Portobello.
Reynald, D. (2010). Guardians on Guardianship: Factors Affecting the Willingness to Supervise, the Ability to Detect Potential Offenders, and the Willingness to Intervene. *Journal of Research in Crime and Delinquency, 47*(3), 358–390.
Richardson, L., Richardson, J., Bradshaw, J., Guest, C., Malovic, A., & Himmerich, J. (2016). "I Felt That I Deserved It"—Experiences and Implications of Disability Hate Crime. *Tizard Learning Disability Review, 21*(2), 80–88.
Roulstone, A., & Mason-Bish, H. (Eds.). (2013). *Disability, Hate Crime and Violence*. Abingdon: Routledge.
Sung-suk, V., Smith, M., & Ceccato, V. (2014). Commuters Using Public Transit in New York City: Using Area-Level Data to Identify Neighbourhoods with Vulnerable Riders (Safety on the Move). *Security Journal, 27*(2), 194–209.
Sykes, G., & Matza, D. (1957). Techniques of Neutralization. In E. McLaughlin & J. Muncie (Eds.) (2013), *Criminological Perspectives* (3rd ed.). London: Sage.
Thornicroft, G., Brohan, E., Rose, D., Sartorius, N., Leese, M., & The INDIGO Study Group. (2009). Global Pattern of Experienced and Anticipated Discrimination Against People with Schizophrenia. *Lancet, 373*, 408–415.
Vaes, J., Leyens, J., Paola Paladino, M., & Pires Miranda, M. (2012). We Are Human, They Are Not: Driving Forces Behind Outgroup Dehumanisation and the Humanisation of the Ingroup. *European Review of Social Psychology, 23*(1), 64–106.
Vilalta, C. (2011). Fear of Crime in Public Transport: Research in Mexico City. *Crime Prevention and Community Safety, 13*(3), 171–186.
Walters, M. (2011). A General Theories of Hate Crime? Strain, Doing Difference and Self Control. *Critical Criminology, 19*(4), 313–330.
Walters, M., Brown, R., & Wiedlitzka, S. (2016). *Causes and Motivations of Hate Crime*. Manchester: Equality and Human Rights Commission.
World Health Organisation (WHO). (2017). *10 Facts on Disability, Updated November 2017*. Online at: http://www.who.int/features/factfiles/disability/en/. Accessed 10 Dec 2018.

CHAPTER 7

Disability Hate Crime on Public Transport: Conclusion and New Directions

Abstract This concluding chapter reflects on the personal research journey taken to reveal the experiences of disability hate crime victims on public transport by the author. The chapter substantiates the methodology used, its original contribution to knowledge and its findings. The chapter then turns towards the future. It discusses the implications for theory and knowledge and what changes have been made because of the author's research. It then asks questions of future research and methodology before citing implications for policy and practice in the UK.

Keywords Reflection • Future directions and policy • Questions for future research

7.1 Chapter Introduction: Looking Back at the Journey

This chapter recaps the journey which my research—and also this book—has taken. Additionally, the chapter presents a set of recommendations designed to shape a more victim-focused policy agenda relating to hate crime on public transport in the UK. The research journey has been convoluted in terms of: realising the impact of the problem; finding the confidence to begin the research; securing personal funding; considering the research structure; conducting the research; interpreting its findings and committing it to writing. For me, this journey began around 45 years ago

D. Wilkin, *Disability Hate Crime*, Palgrave Hate Studies,
https://doi.org/10.1007/978-3-030-28726-9_7

whilst being a victim of disability hate crime (DHC) on public transport during childhood. These experiences proved to latterly be the catalyst for an exploration into what other people with learning difficulties, physical disabilities and mental ill-health have experienced in terms of similar hostility whilst they were using public transport. Finding people who have suffered these experiences and reflecting upon them was the easier part of this research, although much heart-searching and upset was caused along the way. Participants came forward to be listened to, both through interviews and focus groups, some as a result of chance encounters. The more difficult task was gathering data from the authorities and the transport service providers. One specific difficulty was speaking with public transport staff members. They were concerned that they might lose their jobs because they publicly revealed their scarcity of knowledge and confidence in dealing with people with disabilities.

People with, or without, disabilities should be encouraged to use public transport if only because of its positive effect on reducing car use and the independence given to people without alternative transport. Much excellent work is being done to safeguard the travel experiences of people with disabilities, and this should not be overlooked. However, this work is sporadic and disparate. As can be seen from Chap. 5, this work is being performed without clear leadership from central UK government or from most local authorities or regulatory agencies questioned within my study. To shape a victim-centred policy agenda, this chapter will include a discussion of implications concerning theory and research, research methods and implications regarding policy and practice.

7.2 Re-examining the Research Approach

The research objectives were:

- To consider the dynamics between victims, perpetrators and bystanders on public transport.
- To assess which public transport modes pose a greater risk for victims of DHC.
- To explore the impacts of DHC on public transport.
- To examine the ways in which public transport providers and frontline staff respond to DHC on public transport.
- To use research evidence to develop a series of recommendations for policy and practice to improve responses to DHC on public transport.

Hate crime on public transport, a problem which is recognised in the several sources cited within this book, is an under-researched area. I continue to find it difficult to understand why this important area had remained unresearched for so long, a realisation which proved to be one fillip to delve into this world of abuse. This abuse perpetrated within the small environment consisting of relative strangers, which is public transport. The aspiration was, and remains, to make a positive change and thus to make life better for all of those who use public transport, whether disabled or able-bodied. This aspiration generally aligns with that of the Leicester Hate Crime Project's Victim's Manifesto (2014:5). This monograph recommends positive improvements for victims of hate crime, and these are stated in the following text.

My research project did not remain unchallenged or unchanged. Several modifications were made in an attempt to refine both the project and data collection methods. The research question changed on many occasions as did the research objectives. Exploratory studies like mine need not only agile research approaches to reflect new lines of inquiry from interviews but also to embrace inclusivity of a diverse range of people with different needs and communication styles. Changes made during the course of the study were not only to reflect changing approaches and input from those guiding me but also to reflect the inputs of the, disappointingly few, representatives of Deaf and Disabled People's Organisations (DDPOs) who made their time available for this project. Additionally, and perhaps most importantly, recommended changes came from the participants themselves who applied significance to their investment in this project. For example, because of their direction, questioning techniques were adjusted to reflect the emergence of what came to be characterised as Collaborative Alienation Theory. Methods of communication were adjusted to meet the needs of some participants when established methods were either not appropriate or not practicable. Then there was the female participant who wanted to communicate via YouTube and answer questions by email—an example of an adaptation made which also needed to fit within the ethical approval envelope for this project.

Aside from adjustments which were made to accommodate the various disabilities, another consideration was the scope of the project itself. The focus was disability hate crime. Would it not have been better, in the under-researched environment of public transport, that all five recognised strands of hate crime in the UK were researched? The main reasons for the focus on disability were twofold: first that my own disability had attracted hostility initially and this produced a personal interest, and second that disability in itself is a relatively under-researched area. Moreover, to have included all five of the recognised UK hate crime strands (see: Chap. 1, Introduction) may have broadened this work to an unmanageable level and therefore caused the project to no longer be a viable one. The scope of this project could potentially also have widened from public transport out to include other public spaces. This would, however, have created scoping problems in determining which public spaces were to be included and which to exclude. Furthermore, the scope of a project of that size may make it untenable for a single researcher on a limited budget and without sponsorship—which I was. Alternatively, this research could have focused only on bus services where in the light of this research, over 80% of the hate incidents were chronicled. However, this approach would have been too limiting. To properly examine public transport across its many modalities provided a more rounded picture of these facilities. The fact that incidents were not recorded as happening on, for example, aircraft or rivercraft, does not mean to imply that incidents have not occurred therein, merely that participants did not relate experiences on these modes.

Finally, for this section which is reflecting on techniques of scholarship and connecting with disengaged people, the model of disability used is something else which may be questioned. This research, whilst recognising the social model of disability which espouses that it is a society which places obstacles in the way of disabled people and therefore imposes disabilities, chose instead to use the medical model of disability. The medical model asserts that a medical diagnosis is made by a professional and that diagnosis labels the individual and forms the basis of imposed and suggested lifestyle changes from that point forward (see: Chap. 1, Introduction). The decision to use the medical model is not displaying a preference for that model merely that this decision recognises that this model is the one used most widely by the medical profession, social services and the criminal justice system in the UK. It is therefore the one most likely to be recognised in the public transport industry. As this research refers to much documentation which originates from within these organisations, it made little sense to utilise a different form of modality.

7.3 Implications for Theory and Knowledge

The findings within my research broadly align with established, peer-reviewed academic research (see: Chaps. 3, 4, 5 and 6). Specifically, findings concerning the everyday nature of abuse and the ordinariness of hostility against the disabled are generally in agreement with work by Chakraborti et al. (2014), Iganski (2008a, b) and Iganski and Lagou (2015). Findings which refer to the shorter- and longer-term effects of hostility against disabled people are in line with research conducted by Beadle-Brown et al. (2014) and the works of Chakraborti et al. (2014), Clement et al. (2011) and Paterson et al. (2018). The existence of hostility on public transport itself is reflective of work contained within: Chakraborti et al. (2014), the EHRC (2011) and the Home Office (2016). Furthermore, the inaction of most local authorities, regulatory bodies and many service providers in my study aligns with the comments of the Head of the Cross-government Hate Crime Programme (Giannasi 2017) and the Government Equalities Office (2013). For many disabled passengers using public transport, abuse and humiliation are everyday occurrences. Abuse ranged from name-calling to psychological and physical violence, serious assault and serious sexual assault. The distress of abuse has led to disabled people abandoning using public transport—a behaviour which leads to social isolation and missed opportunities. That the findings from the study generally align with established academic work builds confidence in both the strength of the earlier theorisation and the validity of my study. This study has helped to validate earlier thinking whilst moving research into the previously undeveloped area of public transport. Therefore, for criminology, boundaries are evidently being extended.

A catalyst for abuse is often the use, and a refusal to relinquish, wheelchair spaces or priority seating—this was noticeable in 60% of cases. Most abuse is conducted on buses and trams. The principal offender often used formerly unoffending fellow passengers to predicate and exacerbate abuse. Participants reported this phenomenon in 71% of incidents on buses and trams and in 23% of incidents on trains, totalling 52% of participants experiencing this effect overall. An explanatory framework for this phenomenon has been offered, and I have characterised this as Collaborative Alienation Theory (see: Chap. 6). Fellow passengers, aside from those collaborating with the principal offender, mostly chose to ignore any victimisation of disabled passengers and this ignorance also placed victims in distressing situations. In most cases of hostility, whether these involved collaboration or not, staff members were either unwilling or unable to help manage incidents. Both victim participants and public transport staff thought that this was due to ineffective training and an absence of confidence to do so. The implications for hate crime scholarship are therefore clear. The originality of my study has led to a wider understanding of hate crime perpetration, and techniques of offending have been brought to light which are employed in restricted environments. Gesturing, subtle displays of hostility, debilitating comments and employing collaborators have all been frequently illustrated (see: Chap. 3). Whilst the canon of attacking people because of their presumed difference is maintained (e.g., Iganski 2008b), the nuances of the hostility expended in confined spaces add to scholastic understanding and provide tools and insight for further research.

Therefore, although my study was specifically limited to hate crimes and incidents on public transport modes, some of its findings may be generalisable to other social settings. For example, some of the behaviours which occur in the confines of the bus, tram or train might easily be replicated in other small spaces like a café, a communal room, a treatment setting or some other small public building. The emergent Collaborative Alienation Theory is an explanatory framework which has the potential to be transferred to other settings where other ingroup/outgroup interactions might exist. Because of the paucity of research specifically focusing on public transport and the originality of Collaborative Alienation Theory, academic researchers cannot afford to assume that it does not translate into other settings or situations. These explicit factors aside, my study has extended implicit knowledge of the violence which is faced by disabled people on a daily basis; this knowledge has additionally enhanced an understanding of the abuse and the coping mechanisms which may be deployed daily by disabled people or by any other victim of a hate incident. What this research has also achieved is that it has opened the boundaries of hate crime victimisation scholarship and thereby stimulated further debate. This research has uncovered the inaction of national and local governmental organisations and of the EHRC to protect susceptible sections of the citizenry due to them not utilising existing and enforceable legislation. Furthermore, my study has additionally questioned the constraints which social scientists have adopted. To hear the 'lost voices' of unfamiliar victims (Garland et al. 2005:423), researchers may need to explore new methods and extend epistemological boundaries as the following section will discuss.

7.4 Implications for Future Research and Future Methods

This research has called into question the way in which social science typifies groups of people and determines those who are supposedly the hard to reach. As evidenced in Chap. 2, people perceived as vulnerable have been excluded from research. However, the richness of the evidence cited in Chaps. 3 and 4 is surely proof that social scientists need to re-evaluate any reticence towards involving some groups of people. Participants to my study have brought abundant experience along with an eagerness to participate and an interest in improving their lifestyles as well. This is not to suggest that we abandon risk assessments and proper ethical evaluations in research endeavours. However, social scientists may need to re-assess their own partiality in an attempt to reach relatively untapped data sources. Moreover, in the operationalisation of research, researchers could extend boundaries by not being deterred by potential communications difficulties or perceived cultural barriers. In my study, flexible and agile research methods were utilised which incorporated diverse interactions through different media like YouTube, through audio recordings of informed consent and through the inclusion of carers and friends. Research participants to my study actively recommended the adoption of different methods to enable conversation and group work which were readily implemented. Furthermore, my study, through its formula of using grounded theory analysis, has generated Collaborative Alienation Theory. Consequently the combination of approaching an under-researched group of people and the creativity empowered by grounded theory analysis has allowed the production of emergent theorisation. These factors contrive to make my study a groundbreaking one contributing originality to academic knowledge.

Furthermore, there are unexplored permutations which offer much potential for future research within the much used social asset that is public transport. More work may be required to explore the intersectionalities of social harm. A deeper exploration of when staff members are themselves the victims of hate offences may be required or perhaps what effect the quality of staff training has in safeguarding passengers. A wider scope for future research might venture to capture all of the recognised strands of hate crime across public transport. Future research might also tackle the questions of whether there is a predominance to commit crime against females on public transport or whether these crimes might be connected with a socio-economic typology of passengers. Does the route geography make a difference to criminogenesis; in other words, are the places served by that route a contributory factor and does the availability of on-board security make a difference to the effecting of hate offences? Within public transport vehicles, is the propensity for hate crime connected with the seating layout? For example, seats on short-haul buses tend to have a lower back-profile than on trains, and might this affect the actioning of hate offences? Is the risk of hostility increased because of the differing form of compartmentation used on buses? More compartmentation is facilitated on trains to reduce the risk of draught from doors and also for the enforcement of fare zones. Compartmentation could potentially reduce exposure within the one, single open space most often found within buses. What about the escape potential? On a bus it may be almost impossible to affect an escape from any episode of victimisation. On a train, especially a longer one, the victim may be able to move to another carriage. Albeit that some wheelchair-using victims may be limited to wheelchair bays, accessible toilets and other people with disabilities to priority seating. These are all factors which may need to be considered for research by criminologists, psychologists and human geographers to broaden our knowledge of why, when and where offences are likely to occur.

Other implications for future research have become clearer because of my study. More research is needed to further explore and develop the theory of Collaborative Alienation Theory. Research needs to expand on the interactions between the principal offender and other passengers. Not only should the people who are successfully recruited by the principal offender be studied—but additionally the ones who have not succumbed to being so recruited. The interactive behaviours of the principal offender and these potential recruits need to be examined alongside the reactions of those who are observers of this phenomenon. Ideally, principal offenders, recruits and those who declined recruitment need to be subjected to qualitative interviewing to ascertain their motivation for the course of action which they have chosen. Social psychological experimentation might be a viable method through which to study such interactions. If properly developed, Collaborative Alienation Theory might be applied to a range of social situations and hate crime perpetration.

There were many lessons learned from garnering information from a variety of agencies. Freedom of Information (FOI) Act requests and other enquiries were made of the 28 local authorities or Passenger Transport Executives (PTEs) in the areas where victims had reported hate crimes or incidents. Most of the authorities contacted proclaimed that they did not operate public transport themselves having the effect of absolving them from the responsibility of ensuring that disabled people are protected. However, they declined to mention that most of these authorities operate bus stops, bus interchanges and contracted for commercially unviable bus services on Sundays and Bank Holidays, and also for people with specific needs and for school children. Their obligations under equality legislation place with them the responsibility to ensure that statutory equalities are entwined in contractual negotiations and tendering. Many authorities claimed not to hold the information required. This implies that policies, strategies or objectives did not exist within these organisations to ensure that public transport operators adhere to equality legislation. Such policies would have been instrumental in establishing protective frameworks to safeguard disabled passengers on public transport modes. Some evidence of safeguarding equalities was present in only eight authorities: Transport for Greater Manchester, Transport for London, Essex County Council, Brighton and Hove City Council, South Yorkshire PTE, Edinburgh City Council, Gateshead Council, NEXUS and Plymouth City Council. Many authorities confirmed that Disability Awareness Training was in place for staff members in compliance with current legislation. Only one of the authorities responded to confirm that their Public Sector Equality Duty (PSED) was being met.

Not all of the FOI requests were responded to; of those who did respond, some authorities delegated the responsibility for answering questions to a public transport provider. Of the responses received directly from the authority to which the requests were made, most responses were scant and revealed little relating to the questions directly put. Only four authorities responded with detail and rigour meaning that overall the response of authorities in the compliance of their legislative duty was poor (see: Chap. 5 for detail). Moreover, the response of 6 DDPOs from the 66 organisations which were originally approached is a poor reaction from organisations established to care and support susceptible groups within society. This clearly demonstrates that any expectation of cooperation from responsible agencies can be misplaced. However, being ill-served by gatekeepers incentivised a programme of direct recruitment. This, provided that they are ethically rigorous strategies, can evidently be more productive and a more easily controlled method of reaching out to potential participants (see: Chap. 2).

7.5 Implications for Policy and Practice

My study found that whilst legislation exists and policy has been formed to protect the disabled passenger, this rarely translates into effective regimes. Staff members are unaware of how to manage incidents of hostility against disabled passengers and training is, in the main, not adequate to deliver either awareness or managing strategies for coping with this hostility. Providers are ill-equipped to deal with such incidents, and the government maintain a low priority towards assuaging this problem. This section now offers recommendations for future policy direction. These could potentially assist all users of public transport to be safeguarded on their journeys. Policy bodies have access to current legislation—now they additionally have access to the resulting experiences of this legislation not being enforced. Evidence was revealed in Chap. 2 indicating that increased confidence equates to increased ridership. This section latterly also offers speculation as to what might happen if changes do not occur to protect disabled public transport users.

The key findings from my study influence these recommendations. Established bus partnerships and crime reduction partnerships should not incur an additional cost if they include protection of disabled public transport users as recommended herein. The creation and maintenance of equality objectives and sympathetic contractual adjustments by partnerships are comparatively cost-neutral and should be established as a statutory duty. Any action which protects the disabled traveller which is borne out of such partnership working can only be advantageous to all passengers, to society more widely and to the professional reputations of public transport providers. Each of the remaining recommendations, should they be implemented, may however attract a cost. The enforcement, incorporation and application of the Equality Act 2010 and of the PSED in all public transport procurement and service provision applications may be cost-positive, and this perhaps provides an explanation as to why these statutory actions have not been more widely applied to date. The enhancement of the training of front-line staff to Disability Equality Training (DET) standard would also attract a cost. However, with many equality modules available both online and face-to-face and with the availability of group discounts from training providers, it is questionable just how expensive equality and awareness training would be. Moreover, the cost of implementation has been described as minimal by NEXUS in North East England (Lewis 2019). It is noteworthy however that the enhanced reputations of local authorities, regulatory bodies and public transport service providers would only serve to positively enhance reputations, reduce risk and drive down the possibility of judicial action to rectify non-compliance. The following set of recommendations utilises both evidence from within my study and from current legislation and/or regulation. They represent future policy and practice which could potentially safeguard both disabled and non-disabled people alike when using public transport in the UK.

Policing and Best Practice

Many of the victims and witnesses to the study voiced their poor confidence in the reporting of incidents, with only 8% being satisfied with reporting outcomes (see: Chap. 3). The approach to raising awareness of hate crime on the UK rail network by the British Transport Police (BTP) has been proactive as have their robust recording and oversight of hate offences. But whilst other forces have learned from the BTP their approach has not been widely adopted (BTP 2017; HMICFRS 2018). For the BTP, when a hate incident or crime is reported, it is flagged throughout the reporting process as a hate crime and a detective oversees the progression of a sample of reports. The standardisation of the reporting forms has additionally helped the BTP to record and to track hate crimes through the reporting process. A Data Integrity Unit also checks the veracity of this process (BTP 2017). These practices are not consistently operationalised across UK police services (HMICFRS 2018). Therefore, the first recommendation is to adopt these practices in police services across the UK and commit to early flagging of victim- or witness-declared hate crime reports. This could be reinforced by issuing an operational stipulation which requires police officers to do this rather than relying on police officers using discretion as to whether, or not, to follow the College of Policing (CoP 2014) guidance. In doing so, a consistent approach will be followed that is acceptable to the Crown Prosecution Service (CPS 2019).

This level of safeguarding, if not replicated in local police services, could result in the reporting of disability hate crime remaining low, and thus the identification of hate crime overlooked. Furthermore, crime data will not accurately reflect the true picture of hate offences. Moreover, the result of not updating processes may be that the government has restricted access to data and thus remains relatively uncommitted to taking reparatory action to reduce disability hate crime. The BTP also participates in monthly awareness meetings with the public and works with charities and other agencies to promote the awareness of hate crime. They also publish the *We Stand Together* campaign to reduce hate crime which offers clear reporting pathways through a dedicated app, which increased discreet reporting of hate offences by 82% during 2017–18 (The Guardian 2018), using telephone, social media and text messaging services. Hence, the BTP approach could be seen as a clear strategy to be followed by other forces. However, the potential if these approaches are not adopted by local police services across the UK is that awareness of the plight of disabled people as well as other hate crime victims will remain low, and consequently, disabled people will continue to be everyday victims of hate attacks (HMICFRS 2018).

Effective Leadership

Evidence within my study, either from Giannasi (2017) or that demonstrated by the inaction of regulatory authorities or public transport providers signify that regulatory leadership and compliance with legislation is not being effected (Hamilton and Trickett 2014; Chap. 5). The DfT and other governmental agencies need to lead, work more closely and be coordinated in their actions to tackle hate crime generally and the threat of disability hate crime specifically. In other words, these bodies need to show commitment and leadership in accord with the first core recommendation from the EHRC (2011:166). Failure to do so may result in disabled people remaining economically inactive and suffering a rising level of educational needs. If the use of public transport is one way towards reducing an environmental footprint, then these forms of transport should be encouraged. This will not be achieved if people with disabilities, which number up to 19% of the potential users, are dissuaded from using these services by fear of being abused. To assist central and local governmental agencies in determining the future policy directions, the Crime Survey of England and Wales needs to encompass some questions within it regarding disability hate crime and especially the effect on the choice of whether to use public transport or not. Without these data, the dearth of knowledge regarding problem will continue, and consequently, the UK government will not be incentivised to act positively to reduce disability hate crime. An example of clear local authority leadership in this respect is the NEXUS Hate Crime Charter for Public Transport which provides clear partnership arrangements, direction and commitments (Lewis 2019; NEXUS 2018).

Public Transport Staff Training

An overwhelming proportion of the participants in this research had little confidence in public transport staff members being able to recognise or manage hate incidents or know how to report them. Staff members questioned had little knowledge of the rights of disabled people, the potential for them being victims of hostility or how to manage such incidents (see: Chaps. 3 and 5). Therefore, Disability Equality Training should be delivered to public transport front-line staff and supervisors to give them the tools to recognise and help to manage incidents of hostility aboard their vehicles. This training should also be fully evaluated to ensure that it is effective. For this assessment to occur, customer survey regimes would need to be adapted to incorporate feedback from disabled passengers. The *one-size-fits-all* approach to passenger surveys which do not reflect the specific views of disabled passengers is therefore not an inclusive measure (see: Chap. 5). Effective and evaluated training would align with the EHRC (2018) guidance that:

> *Public transport providers and regulators across Britain should work together … to ensure that all staff members have the knowledge and skills to meet the needs of disabled passengers.* (EHRC 2018:209)

Authorities should also insist that this is embedded in all contractual arrangements and when tendering for bids to operate services—as demanded by the PSED. Service providers should embed this training in their recruitment and annual licencing refresher activities. This form of training will give awareness of accessibility expectations as well as the human rights of disabled travellers. This training can only help to improve the national and international repute of global public transport providers. This training aligns directly with one of the seven core recommendations within EHRC (2011:167) which asserts that front-line staff members are essential in recognition of hostility and need training to help in this regard. Furthermore, the DfT is working towards providing an accreditation scheme for transport operators to receive 'formal recognition for work to improve disabled passengers' experiences' (DfT 2018a: online). Moreover, NEXUS in the Tyne and Wear area have produced a Hate Crime Charter for Public Transport providing direction, support and clarity for training and for raising awareness in staff (Lewis 2019; NEXUS 2018).

Legislative Failures

Evidence within my study has highlighted the muddled picture that regulatory and local authorities provided towards their responsibilities and how they discharge these (see: Chap. 5). Local authorities, regulatory agencies and bus partnerships must fully comply with their responsibilities within current legislation to provide safeguarded travel for all of its passengers—inclusive of those with disabilities. They should take leadership on equality issues during the provision, procurement and delivery of public transport facilities—as required by the PSED. Agencies should take their responsibilities to produce and monitor equality objectives seriously and so too their obligation to produce an annual appraisal of these activities. Activities in support of equality legislation will also promote positivity towards disabled people in accord with core recommendation five of EHRC (2011:167). Not to do so would leave any attempt to improve the lives of people with disabilities unaudited. To ensure that compliance is undertaken, the EHRC needs to diligently fulfil its obligations, which include:

> *Intervening in strategic cases that raise important issues under either the equality law, human rights law or both.*
>
> *Raising proceedings for judicial review in our own name in strategic cases that raise important issues under either the equality law, human rights law or both.*
>
> *Conducting inquiries and investigations.*
>
> *Conducting assessments into the extent to which a public authority has complied with the public sector equality duty.* (EHRC 2018:43)

Furthermore, guidance from the DfT (2018b) prompts public transport providers to address equality issues and to raise awareness generally concerning disability hate crime. It also suggests that public transport staff members from the back office to the front-line need to be aware of equality issues. But it falls short of training staff as to how to manage incidents of hostility and how to report these. Aside from this, the guidance promises that the UK government will monitor complaints from disabled people using these services. But this measurement will be of limited use if the victims continue to not, in the main, report these incidents. Lastly, it avoids compelling local authorities from incorporating their PSED duties in the contracting and influence they have over public transport providers.

Third-party Reporting

Participants within my study voiced their frustrations at not being confident to report incidents or being in fear of the consequences of reporting (see: Chap. 3). Awareness of third-party reporting (TPR) capabilities should be widened to public transport staff as a confidential avenue to reporting hate crime with the confidence that these reports will be progressed. TPR should be facilitated by fully trained individuals in secure and comfortable settings to enhance effectiveness and confidence in TPR generally. To provide these support mechanisms would align with core recommendation six of EHRC (2011:167). Not to do so would leave the burden of reporting solely with the police who are arguably already overworked and under-resourced. Accumulated data gathered through TPR avenues would augment that already in the public arena and could only add value to the range of knowledge and understanding of such crimes. There would not necessarily be a cost here as many charity organisations are now empowered to solicit TPR reports—Victim Support and Stop Hate UK are just two examples.

Prosecution Protocol

The CPS should remove from its protocols the acceptance that perceived 'vulnerability' on the part of the defendant is a reason for not uplifting sentences (CPS 2018:11).

> *Some offenders are motivated by a perception that disabled people are 'vulnerable' or an 'easy target', rather than by hostility or hatred. This is an important distinction and the CPS is unable to apply for statutory sentence uplift under the Criminal Justice Act 2003 in these cases.* (CPS 2018:11)

Albeit that this approach does make the prosecution more viable (CPS 2019) and although the Law Commission (2018) is reviewing prosecution strategy and legislation regarding hate offences, participants to my study felt that the law does not provide enough recognition and protection for their victimisation (see: Chap. 3). Therefore, in support of the recommendations cited above, prosecutions should reflect the nature and impact of hate offences.

Wider Considerations

In policy terms, any application of the above recommendations should also be thought of in wider terms. Any promotion which leads to an uptake of ridership of public transport services can only be of an environmental benefit to local authorities in striving to meet their environmental impact targets. Moreover, any reduction in the amount of road traffic can only be beneficial regarding infrastructure damage, and only economic positivity can be gained from fewer delays to travel. The willingness to fully discharge statutory responsibilities in a UK where this legislation is rarely enforced is unlikely to be forthcoming unless sanctions begin to apply to those agencies which fail to comply with legislation (Giannasi 2017).

7.6 Summarising the Conclusion

Reflecting on the research journey, this research is a testament to the power of victimisation which lingers throughout a victim's life leaving a stain embedded in one's conscience forever. Much of the evidence from participants was collected through tears of discomfort, often produced by the participant and sometimes by myself. The emotion of meeting people who had suffered the same fate was palpable. These experiences occurred in different places from mine and decades apart, but the effect was the same. I also witnessed the joy which some participants displayed revealing some inner pain which they perhaps thought would never see the light of day again. Generally, participants were glad that these experiences were being revealed and the message from them was to make sure that others were aware of their ordeals.

This research has answered a need. It has conducted research and asked questions which had previously remained unasked. It has revealed horrifying levels of abuse and violence which have been occasioned—and still are being occasioned—against disabled people every day on the public transport networks of the UK. It has asked questions of those agencies which authorise, license or procure public transport and which have a responsibility for instilling in those services the types of equality measures which might potentially make life better for the disabled traveller. This work has discovered that these regulators, in the main, do not apply the level of seriousness which is expected of responsible public bodies to safeguard disabled public transport users. This derogation begins at the top. The UK government is not considering disability hate crime as a priority. This attitude of the government, local authorities and regulators permeates down to those who are charged with providing the services. Therefore, although well reported that public transport modes are as areas of criminogenesis for the disabled passenger, this threat is left unmanaged.

It was not difficult however to find the experiences of those who have suffered this hostility. Nonetheless, it was difficult to ascertain exactly what governing agencies were doing to alleviate it. When these answers were found, they equated to ***not much***. The front-line staff who need to be aware of, and manage, these incidents on a daily basis mostly avoided doing so. They do not generally do this out of spite but out of ignorance as to what to do to help their passengers. This culmination of governmental ignorance, provider avoidance and staff unfamiliarity is leaving up to 19% of the UK population (World Health Organisation [WHO] 2017) potentially without the means to safely and securely travel independently and without fear and lead the kind of lives which the rest of the population reasonably take for granted. The option to do something about this situation does exist—but will it ever be used?

Therefore, whilst there is the joy of seeing all of these collected experiences on the written page, there is also a foreboding of what comes next: a continuation of this work, a cessation, an unknown? My study has not been restricted to gathering data and forming this into an academic monograph. I have additionally consulted with a range of stakeholders representing the UK government, the public transport industry and those who support disabled people. Regular public lectures were held with organisations which fight for disability rights or fight hate crime. Academic lectures were convened to engage the academic community in what was ostensibly a new conceptual area of study. I was recruited onto working parties and steering groups which formulate public transport policy and advisory groups for franchise bids. I was successful in collaborating with Essex County Council to incorporate hate crime awareness training into the annual refresher and re-licensing training for bus staff across that county, one of the largest in the UK. I also have an aspiration to produce a monograph on this topic and publish in appropriate academic journals. However, it is important for the confidence of all users of public transport going forward that the work does not end here. The difficulties of the research journey included learning to write academically for someone who could not form a sentence when leaving a poorly attended school at 16. Surprised at how transformations are so quickly made, I moved from someone embedded in the public transport industry to someone who could speak confidently about criminology and about hate crime in particular. This was necessary to fully engage with professionals who have been in the criminal justice system and academic criminology for many years. But these were only small steps, on a long, long road.

Bibliography

Beadle-Brown, J., Richardson, L., Guest, C., Malovic, A., Bradshaw, J., & Himmerich, J. (2014). *Living in Fear: Better Outcomes for People with Learning Disabilities and Autism, Main Research Report.* Canterbury: Tizard Centre, University of Kent.

British Transport Police (BTP). (2017, August 3). *Interview Between the Author and Inspector Granville Sellers, Deputy Lead for Hate Crimes, of the BTP Safeguarding Hub.* Leeds: British Transport Police.

Chakraborti, N., Garland, J., & Hardy, S.-J. (2014). *The Leicester Hate Crime Project: Findings and Conclusions.* Leicester: University of Leicester.

Clement, S., Brohan, E., Sayce, L., Pool, J., & Thornicroft, G. (2011). Disability Hate Crime, Targeted Violence and Hostility: A Mental Health and Discrimination Perspective. *Journal of Mental Health, 20*(3), 219–225.

College of Policing (CoP). (2014). *Hate Crime Operational Guidance.* Coventry: College of Policing.

Crown Prosecution Service (CPS). (2018). *Hate Crime Annual Report 2017–18.* London: The Crown Prosecution Service.

Crown Prosecution Service (CPS). (2019, February 14). *Interview Between the Researcher and Mick Conboy, Hate Crime Stakeholder Manager: Operations Directorate, Crown Prosecution Service.* London: The Crown Prosecution Service.

Department for Transport. (2018a). *Next Steps Towards a Fully Inclusive Transport Network.* Online at: https://www.gov.uk/government/news/next-steps-towards-a-fully-inclusive-transport-network. Accessed 3 Jan 2019.

Department for Transport. (2018b). *The Inclusive Transport Strategy: Achieving Equal Access for Disabled People.* London: Department for Transport.

Equality and Human Rights Commission (EHRC). (2011). *Hidden in Plain Sight: Inquiry into Disability-Related Harassment.* Manchester: Equality and Human Rights Commission.

Equality and Human Rights Commission (EHRC). (2018). *Is Britain Fairer? The State of Equality and Human Rights 2018.* Manchester: Equality and Human Rights Commission.

Garcia, V. (2018, March 9). *An Interview Between the Author and Victoria Garcia, Accessibility and Communities Manager for Brighton and Hove Buses and Metrobus.*

Garland, J., Spalek, B., & Chakraborti, N. (2005). Hearing Lost Voices: Issues in Researching 'Hidden' Minority Ethnic Communities. *British Journal of Criminology, 46*, 423–437.

Giannasi, P. (2017, September 20). *Interview at the Home Office Between the Author and Paul Giannasi Head of the Cross-Government Hate Crime Programme.*

Guardian (The). (2018, January 25). Less Than 25% of Hate Crime Reports on UK Railways Lead to Charges. *The Guardian* (online). London: The Guardian. Online at: https://www.theguardian.com/uk-news/2018/dec/25/hate-crime-reports-uk-railways-charges-british-transport-police-figures. Accessed 10 Jan 2019.

Hamilton, P., & Trickett, L. (2014). Disability Hostility, Harassment and Violence in the UK: A 'Motiveless' and 'Senseless' Crime? In N. Hall, A. Corb, & P. Giannasi (Eds.), *Routledge International Handbooks: Routledge International Handbook on Hate Crime* (pp. 207–225). New York: Routledge.

Her Majesties Inspectorate of Constabulary and Fire & Rescue Services (HMICFRS). (2018). *Understanding the Difference: The Initial Police Response to Hate Crime*. London: Her Majesties Inspectorate of Constabulary and Fire & Rescue Services.

HM Government Equalities Office. (2013). *The Independent Steering Group's Report of the Public Sector Equality Duty (PSED): Review and Government Response*. Online at: https://www.gov.uk/government/publications/the-independent-steering-groups-report-of-the-public-sector-equality-duty-psed-review-and-government-response. Accessed 14 July 2017.

Home Office. (2016). *Action Against Hate: The UK Government's Plan for Tackling Hate Crime*. London: Home Office.

Iganski, P. (2008a). *Hate Crime and the City*. Bristol: The Policy Press.

Iganski, P. (2008b). Criminal Law and the Routine Activity of 'Hate Crime'. *Liverpool Law Review, 29*(1), 1–17.

Iganski, P., & Lagou, S. (2015). The Personal Injuries of 'Hate Crime'. In N. Hall, A. Corb, & P. Giannasi (Eds.), *Routledge International Handbooks: Routledge International Handbook on Hate Crime* (pp. 34–46). New York: Routledge.

Law Commission (The). (2018). *Law Commission Review into Hate Crime Announced*. London: The Law Commission. Online at: https://www.lawcom.gov.uk/law-commission-review-into-hate-crime-announced/. Accessed 28 Oct 2018.

Leicester Hate Crime Project's Victim's Manifesto. (2014). Leicester: University of Leicester.

Lewis, H. (2019, March 15). *Interview Between the Author and Huw Lewis, Customer Services Director of NEXUS*.

Mason-Bish, H. (2015). Beyond the Silo: Rethinking Hate Crime and Intersectionality. In N. Hall, A. Corb, & P. Giannasi (Eds.), *Routledge International Handbooks: Routledge International Handbook on Hate Crime* (pp. 24–33). New York: Routledge.

NEXUS. (2018). *Hate Crime Charter for Public Transport, Tyne and Wear: NEXUS*. Online at: https://www.nexus.org.uk/sites/default/files/hate_crime_charter_for_public_transport.pdf. Accessed 17 Dec 2018.

Paterson, J., Brown, R., & Walters, M. (2018). The Short and Longer Term Impacts of Hate Crimes Experienced Directly, Indirectly, and Through the Media. *Personality & Social Psychology Bulletin*, 1–17.

World Health Organisation (WHO). (2017). *10 Facts on Disability, Updated November 2017*. Online at: http://www.who.int/features/factfiles/disability/en/. Accessed 10 Mar 2018.

Index

D. Wilkin, *Disability Hate Crime*, Palgrave Hate Studies,
https://doi.org/10.1007/978-3-030-28726-9